Thoughts After midnight: Information you won't find in the mass media.

CHAPTER ONE

The Wheel

Trying to describe what is happening in the world today seems like an impossible task. But when all the pieces are put together somewhat like a puzzle, it's really rather simple if you have all of the pieces, and if you can put these pieces together in an understandable way or model.

For this article, let's mind play using a great wheel as the model. Imagine this wheel rolling downhill for many years, a wheel that cannot be stopped by human means, a wheel that has become so complex that even the many so called experts cannot figure it out or stop it.

At the very center of the hub of this wheel is the spirit of Satan. This spirit is the motivator that gives the wheel movement and direction. Listed around the hub are the few World Bankers, the really big money people, the movers and shakers of the financial world that are known by but few people and who live in the shadows. Under their influence are the thousands of banks that exist in the world. Their objective we will get to later, but first let's identify the players.

This wheel has many spokes and each spoke has a name. These spokes are the facilitators, the tools used by those at the top to accomplish goals, to control governments and governmental leaders, to start and stop wars, to control money supply, to control the price of oil, fuel, and food. Listed below are the names of each spoke:

The United Nations

The Federal Reserve System

The World Bank

The Bilderburg Group

The Tri-Lateral Commission

The Counsel on Foreign Relations

The Masonic Brotherhood

The Jesuit Society

The Club of Rome

The Skull and Bones Society

The Illuminati

The Knights of Malta

The Royal Institute of International Affairs

Each of these groups have off-shoots in various countries with various names that are almost, but not impossible, to trace. Most top governmental leaders belong to one or more of these secret societies.

You can find out who they are by going to the web.

Their objective is to establish a cashless, socialist, one world government that will be a platform for a one world leader who for a short time will solve the world's problems and bring peace to the Middle East. A short time later, this leader will turn into a dictator who will enslave the world. This will be the Anti-Christ.

Under the rim of this wheel are the masses of the general public. Many will be run over by this wheel. Those who choose to follow this one world leader will live for awhile, but in the afterlife will suffer great anguish for eternity. Those who choose not to follow this leader, unless they are Raptured, will be killed in one way or another, but will live again with new bodies with Christ when He returns.

This present Administration is trying its best to place government above the Constitution and the Bill of Rights. The Health Care bill is just one more step in taking control of America, even when the majority are against this bill.

If enough people will flood Congress with protests, we may be able to defeat this bill, and throw a kink in Satan's plan to take over America. We may not be able to stop a one world government from becoming a reality, but neither do we need to make it easy for those working toward it - Greyeagle.

A Cup too full

Biblical history has shown that when a nation's cup of iniquity becomes full, God destroys that nation! Examples: The Pre-flood World. Sodom and Gomorrah. Canaan - before the Israelites took possession. Israel, - destroyed by the Assyrians. Judah - destroyed by Babylon. Babylon - destroyed by the Medes and Persians. Persia - destroyed by the Greeks. The Greeks destroyed by Rome. Germany - destroyed by coalition forces. Japan - destroyed by the U.S, and so on?

For hundreds of years, Catholic and Protestant clerics have said the Ten Commandments were nailed to the cross. This explains why most Christians today see no reason to be concerned about keeping them. If we could reason from cause to effect, we would immediately recognize that our world finds itself in a dismal state due to lawlessness.

Parents have not taught their children the importance of man's laws, not to mention the higher laws of God. When the importance of law and obedience is neglected in childhood, moral absolutes disappear and another law, the law of the jungle, prevails. In this jungle of evil, the strongest players rule by force with guns, deceit or whim.

The United States has incarcerated more people than any other developed nation. Why?

When the beauty and necessity of law is ignored in childhood, lawlessness takes over. Sometimes even by those who are sworn to uphold the law. Safety, virtue, and nobility of character disappear when lawlessness rules.

Painful suffering, broken relationships, greed, envy, jealousy, drugs, sexual depravity, and needless deaths are evidences of lawlessness. When the beacon of moral law declines, decadence, chaos, and misery overtakes a society. This cause to effect progression explains why God has had to destroy civilizations from time to time.

When the cup of a nation's iniquity becomes full, total destruction is the only solution. When a nation's non-believers reaches the majority count, leaving only a minority of Christians, God is subject to remove His safety blanket from that nation.

Presently, we are free to believe or disbelieve in an almighty God and to keep all ten of His commandments. If we are not Raptured, there is soon coming a time when we as a people will have only two choices. During the Tribulation, a disastrous time - a time like nothing this world has seen or will ever see again - we will have to choose between the message of God's 144 thousand Spirit filled servants or the messages made into laws by the coalition of religious (Babylon reborn) forces.

Either choice will be a life or death choice for most of the world's population. If we choose the Gospel preached by the 144 thousand servants of God, most of us will be martyred, but will live again with Christ. Some Christ will hide. If we take the side of Babylon (the church of Anti-Christ), we will die horrible deaths at the coming of Christ and for all eternity.

Either way, it's going to be a rough row to hoe! The difference is between life eternal in great happiness with Christ, or suffering life eternal with Satan and his minions. I pray those who read this will take heed to these words and understand what is soon coming, and pray that we will be among those Raptured or that Christ hides us during the Tribulation.

God has been patient for 6000 years because He is giving people time to repent and choose His side. His patience will soon wear thin.

There is soon coming a terrible time of suffering and persecution, and the church is not prepared for these times. Believers have been spoon-fed feel-good sermons so long they are like the people during Noah's time. Noah worked at building his escape boat for 130 years. The people had 130 years to repent and climb aboard the Arc before the flood came. But they didn't repent. All of a sudden water gushed up from below and above and they drowned! They were not prepared!

And neither are we! Today is not a time to wait. It is time to get our business straight with the Creator because a flood is on the way. Not a flood of water, but a flood of persecution! We won't be able to depend upon the government because the government will be the agency that persecutes us. There is no way to soft-peddle this message. It is, in fact, an Ezekiel Warning! This nation's cup is almost full - Greyeagle.

And Lady Liberty Cried

Even the people of Russia are shaking their heads at what Obama and his administration are doing to this country.

However, the wounds are self-inflicted as America elected Obama. But here is an article from the Russian Pravada by Stanislav Mishin titled: American capitalism gone with a whimper. In our defense, America really has not had capitalism - at least in a more true sense of the word - for many decades. But the majority of his observations are accurate.

"It must be said, that like the breaking of a great dam, the American fall into Marxism is happening with breath taking speed, against the back drop of a passive, hapless sheeple, excuse me dear reader, I meant people.

"True, the situation has been well prepared on and off for the past century, especially the past twenty years. The initial testing ground was conducted upon our Holy Russia and a bloody test it was. But we Russians would not just roll over and give up our freedoms and our souls, no matter how much money Wall Street poured into the fists of the Marxists.

"Those lessons were taken and used to properly prepare the American populace for the surrender of their freedoms and souls, to the whims of their elites and betters.

"First, the population was dumbed down through a politicized and substandard education system based on pop culture, rather than the classics. Americans know more about their favorite TV dramas then the drama in DC that directly affects their lives. They care more for their "right" to choke down a McDonalds burger or a BurgerKing burger than for their constitutional rights. Then they turn around and lecture us about our rights and about our "democracy". Pride blind the foolish.

"Then their faith in God was destroyed, until their churches, all tens of thousands of different "branches and denominations" were for the most part little more than Sunday circuses and their televangelists and top protestant mega preachers were more than happy to sell out their souls and flocks to be on the "winning" side of one pseudo Marxist politician or another.

7

Their flocks may complain, but when explained that they would be on the "winning" side, their flocks were ever so quick to reject Christ in hopes for earthly power. Even our Holy Orthodox churches are scandalously liberalized in America.

"The final collapse has come with the election of Barack Obama. His speed in the past three months has been truly impressive. His spending and money printing has been a record setting, not just in America's short history but in the world.

If this keeps up for more than another year, and there is no sign that it will not, America at best will resemble the Wiemar Republic and at worst Zimbabwe.

"These past two weeks have been the most breath taking of all. First came the announcement of a planned redesign of the American Byzantine tax system, by the very thieves who used it to bankroll their thefts, loses and swindles of hundreds of billions of dollars. These make our Russian oligarchs look little more than ordinary street thugs, in comparison. Yes, the Americans have beaten our own thieves in the shear volumes. Should we congratulate them?

"These men, of course, are not an elected panel but made up of appointees picked from the very financial oligarchs and their henchmen who are now gorging themselves on trillions of American dollars, in one bailout after another. They are also usurping the rights, duties and powers of the American congress (parliament). Again, congress has put up little more than a whimper to their masters.

"Then came Barack Obama's command that GM's (General Motor) president step down from leadership of his company. That is correct, reader, in the land of "pure" free markets, the American president now has the power, the self given power, to fire CEOs and we can assume other employees of private companies, at will. Come hither, go dither, the centurion commands his minions.

"So it should be no surprise that the American president has followed this up with a "bold" move of declaring that he and another group of unelected, chosen stooges will now redesign the entire automotive industry and will even be the guarantee of automobile policies.

I am sure that if given the chance, they would happily try and redesign it for the whole of the world, too. Prime Minister Putin, less than two months ago, warned Obama and UK's Blair, not to follow the path to Marxism, it only leads to disaster. Apparently, even though we suffered 70 years of this Western sponsored horror show, we know nothing, as foolish, drunken Russians, so let our "wise" Anglo-Saxon fools find out the folly of their own pride.

"Again, the American public has taken this with barely a whimper but a "freeman" whimper.

"So, should it be any surprise to discover that the democratically controlled Congress of America is working on passing a new regulation that would give the American Treasury department the power to set "fair" maximum salaries, evaluate performance and control how private companies give out pay raises and bonuses? Senator Barney Franks, a social pervert basking in his homosexuality (of course, amongst the modern, enlightened American societal norm, as well as that of the general West, homosexuality is not only not a looked down upon life choice, but is often praised as a virtue) and his Marxist enlightenment, has led this effort. He stresses that this only affects companies that receive government monies, but it is retroactive and taken to a logical extreme, this would include any company or industry that has ever received a tax break or incentive.

"The Russian owners of American companies and industries should look thoughtfully at this and the option of closing their facilities down and fleeing the land of the Red as fast as possible. In other words, divest while there is still value left.

"The proud American will go down into his slavery without a fight, beating his chest and proclaiming to the world, how free he really is. The world will only snicker."

Part of the whole Obama campaign image was that Obama would represent something new and fresh. But what many people don't seem to realize is that there is nothing new about Obama's ideas. They either come straight out of the radicalism of the 1960s or the progressives of the 1930s. Everything the Democrats would like to do in America has already been tried in the old Soviet Union. From nationalization, wage caps, protectionism, government provided health-care and education/indoctrination, etc. It's all been tried before and will have the same disastrous results - economic stagnation, a lower standard of living, and a great loss of liberty. Do we really want America to go down that same road in history? Greyeagle.

The Dream

I saw myself on a high plateau looking down on a plain. I was dressed like the ancient Cherokee of the early 1700's. The Pinto I sat on was sturdy and strong. Except for buckskin trousers and a deer skin vest I was bare above the waist. A quiver was strapped to my back and a bow crossed my chest. On my side was a knife with an antler handle. I carried a spear.

Down below, I saw an Indian, spear in hand, about to face off with a buffalo bull who was about to charge. The Indian began to charge the buffalo at top speed. The buffalo charged, head down, full of fury. I wondered who would be the winner in this battle of wills.

But just as the two combatants reached each other, the charging buffalo disappeared into thin air. The Indian rode right through where the buffalo had been. Sitting there on my high place I wondered where the buffalo had gone?

A cloudy mist erased that scene. An eagle flew close and said: "Now see where the buffalo went: " I looked below and saw hundreds of buffalo stretched as far as the eye could see.

They all had been skinned and their carcasses lay rotting in the sun. My heart was sad because the buffalo was no longer. I wondered how the Indians could survive without the buffalo?

The cloudy mist erased that scene. And I saw hundreds of white buffalo hunters with .50 caliber Sharps rifles sitting down - killing the buffalo for their skins. The air was filled with a putrid smell that made me gag. They took no meat, just the skins. My heart was heavy for the buffalo. My heart cried for the plains Indians who killed only what they needed for food and shelter. The buffalo hunters killed for money.

The mist erased that scene and the majestic eagle said "Come! Let me show you the white man's greatest sin - the greed for land and gold. " Below I saw tribe after tribe, nation after nation, driven from their homelands. I saw men, women and children killed for gold and land. I saw the thousands of peoples who were here many centuries before the white man ever set foot on this soil - was tricked, driven, and herded, onto reservations where they became a downtrodden entity without pride, without hope. I cried, but no tears fell.

The cloudy mist erased that scene and I saw my own people, the Cherokee, driven from their mountain homes and lands in what is now called North Carolina, Tennessee and bordering states. In the middle of winter they were herded like cattle to a far off place called Oklahoma Territory. Thousands died along the way. But some escaped, hid in mountain caves, and became what today is called the Easter Band of the Cherokee Nation. That forced march is called 'The Trail Where They Cried' or 'The Trail of Tears." Those Cherokees that reached Oklahoma Territory became the Western Band of the Cherokee Nation.

The mist erased that scene and I saw a Great White Throne where God, the Great Holy Spirit, will judge the living and the dead in a time to come. Every fiber of my being wanted to feel hatred, resentment, and revenge toward all those who in times past and present who have harmed my people. But I could not. I felt only sorrow and pity. I raised my arms and asked the Great Holy Spirit to forgive those who harmed my people because they were ignorant of the consequences of their actions. I prayed for their souls.

When I awoke, I went to my computer to put my dream to words and I saw my profile picture. Now I know why I am on my Pinto with arms raised. I am praying for those who have harmed my people. I want no revenge, only justice - Greyeagle!

The Real Reason For war In Syria

Syria, is the fertile crescent, the birth place of humanity and civilization. During the ministry of St. Peter Christianity was introduced in Damascus. Syria is home to 21 million people and seven major political groups - Alawites, Sunnis, Christians, Kurds, Shia, Druze, and Arabs. Syria is a diverse and cultured society with world class universities.

The post World War II period was a renaissance for Syria economically. Syria's Gross Domestic Product (GDP) grew by 80% in the 1960's and 336% in the 1970's. Syria exports 650,000 barrels of oil per day and natural gas reservoirs are world class. Average per capita income as late as 2011 grew 3.68%, but in 2012 with civil war GDP has fallen 25%. Seventy thousand civilians have died in the fighting, oil and gas pipelines are being sabotaged by the rebels, and sanctions from the United States and the rest of the world are killing the Syrian economy. Syria has lost its charm.

Barack Hussein Obama campaigned for President in 2008 vowing to end wars in the Muslim world. He has resisted calls by Senators John McCain (R-AZ) and Lindsey Graham (R-SC) to intervene in Syria's ever-more-bloody civil war. Most recently a purported gas attack in an eastern suburb of Damascus has raised the specter of intervention by the United States. The 1,000 or so suspected gas victims has raised the ire of Barack Hussein Obama, but curiously not the 70,000 victims who died by 7.62mm x 39 carbine rounds. Lest you be fooled again by King Obama, any attack on Syria will not be based on humanitarian reasons. He will intervene because Syria has a bad case of gas.

There are two teams in Syria vying for Liquid Natural Gas (LNG) shipments to Europe and China. Team A is the United States, Qatar, Iraq, Turkey, and Israel. They want to build an LNG pipeline from Qatar through Saudi Arabia and Iraq to the Turkish border. Team B is Iran, Iraq, Syria, Russia, Pakistan, and China. They want to build a pipeline from Iran to the Syrian Mediterranean coast (The Islamic Pipeline). Iran would also like to pump Syrian gas through Pakistan into China.

Syria, Israel, Lebanon, Palestinian Authority, and Cyprus share a claim of a recently discovered offshore natural gas reservoir (The Leviathon), which is estimated at 122 trillion cu ft (122 x 1012 cu ft) of available natural gas. Israel obviously wants to claim all of The Leviathon and sell that gas to Europe.

Syria wants to claim all of The Leviathon and sell that gas to Europe, Pakistan, and China.

The world's largest natural gas reservoir is shared by Qatar and Iran. The South Pars (500 x 1012 cu ft) natural gas reservoir has reserves of 500 trillion cu ft. The Iranians have invested heavily on LNG facilities and a pipeline through Pakistan over the past decade to sell this gas to Europe and China.

The energy starved Chinese are said to have funded the hurried construction of the pipeline through Pakistan to their southern border and have agreed to rebuild damaged gas infrastructure if the al-Assad government beats the Syrian rebels. The Russian's have inked deals to their benefit with The Islamic Pipeline and have stationed war ships in the Syrian ports of Tartus and Latakia to protect that investment. We installed a Shite government in Iraq that is allied with Iran. In 2010 Iraq signed a Memorandum of Understanding to allow The Islamic Pipeline to cross its territory.

The opposing Team A is not keen on seeing its natural gas interests interfered with by The Islamic Pipeline. Turkey has always coveted the role of being the major bridge of oil and gas to the East and West, while Qatar wants to monopolize the South Pars reserves. The financial implications are enormous and it's no wonder Team A and Team B will stop at nothing to win their gas war. Syria is the unlucky guy stuck in the middle seat between two guys with gas.

Syria has a huge population of rank-n-file Sunni Muslims. Sunni's hate Alawite Arabs (A Sunni Sect) just a tad less than Shia Muslims and Zionist's. Bashar al-Assad is the President of Syria and a member of the Alawite sect and leader of the Socialist Baath Party of Syria. The rebels are primarily Sunni from Saudi Arabia, Libya, Qatar, and Iraq, a very convenient fact for Qatar and Saudi Arabia.

Qatar and Saudi Arabia are paying to arm the rebels, which contain elements of Al-Qaeda. Turkey is cooperating and allowing those weapons to cross the unpopulated Turkish Syrian border. The United States is threatening to intervene on behalf of the Al-Qaeda rebels with strategic strikes on Assad's military forces. Russia, China, and Iran are warning of strikes on Israel if the United States intervenes. What a mess!

At the time this article was being sent for publication Barack Hussein Obama has indicated he is going to consult with Congress before intervening. Good idea since any intervention by Barack Hussein Obama will violate the Authorization to Use Military Force (AUMF) of 2001, the Constitution of 1789, and The War Powers Act of 1971.

The AUMF identified Al-Qaeda as the seditious organization on which the President was authorized to use military force. If Barack Hussein Obama bombs the al-Assad government it will be assisting Al-Qaeda in violation of the AUMF. He has no authority to initiate military force on the al-Assad government. A war without the express authorization or a Declaration of War by Congress will be in violation of Article 1, Section 8 of the United States Constitution. The Constitution states; "Congress shall have power to ... declare War".

The President has no authority to start a war. The President does have authority by The War Powers Act of 1971 to use force if there is a direct threat to the United States. Within 60 days he must get Congress' approval to continue that military force. Syria is no threat to the United States, so he can't use The War Powers Act as a justification for intervention.

If Barack Hussein Obama bombs Syria and starts another war without Congressional approval, he should be immediately impeached for high crimes and misdemeanors. But this leads to a more profound question. Syria and the Middle East is a mess.

Why do we want to help Al-Qaeda in Syria, while bombing Al-Qaeda in Yemen. These rebels are people who eat the organs of their vanquished enemies, kill Christians, and gas innocent women and children.

Why stick our nose in this stench?

In no particular order:

One: Give the appearance of unifying the country behind the President, who "did his job the right way," by going to Congress for approval. This elevates Obama's ratings and, by inference, suggests that his other programs should be accorded more merit. A wartime president always gains more support.

Two: Give the people an adrenaline rush. The effect should never be underestimated. Cleanses the pores, cleans the slate, and relieves frustration by proxy, temporarily...if you have very little access to your cerebral functions.

Three: In this case, winning Congressional approval reinstates the illusion, for a few moments, that we are a Constitutional Republic, with a government dedicated to justice.

CHAPTER TWO

Four: Help fulfill the long-planned US-Israeli agenda of destabilizing Syria and causing it to partition into warring and chaotic ethnic factions.

Five: Stop the construction of a natural gas pipeline across Syria, which would boost Iran's economy by sending Iranian gas to Europe. Iran's economy must be torpedoed.

Six: Send a message throughout the Middle East that the US is all-powerful and the dollar must remain the reserve currency in all oil transactions.

Seven: Feed the US military-industrial complex, which demands wars.

Eight: Aid the long-term goal of Globalism/Free Trade, which involves putting the entire Middle East into un-resolvable debt and suffering...and then coming in with outside elite bankster financing, to rebuild the entire region and own it, lock, stock, and barrel.

Nine: Distract Americans from a number of scandals, including: Benghazi, Fast&Furious, IRS non-profit division crimes, NSA spying, the continuing failed war in Afghanistan, and a tanking domestic economy with more and more people living below the poverty line.

None of these reasons has anything to do with "punishing Assad for using chemical weapons." In any case, that whole scenario has been thrown into extreme doubt.

Your government at work.

Why Syria?

As Western military forces congregate in the Eastern Mediterranean Sea in anticipation of a "limited strike" on Syria, it is time to ask ourselves a simple question: Why?

In the summer of 2011, just weeks after civil war broke out in Syria, the Tehran Times released a report entitled, Iran, Iraq, Syria Sign Major Gas Pipeline Deal. The report provided details on how Iran planned to export its vast natural gas reserves to Europe through a pipeline that traversed both Iraq and Syria. This Iran-Iraq-Syria pipeline would be the largest gas pipeline in the Middle East and would span from Iran's gas-rich South Pars field to the Mediterranean coastline in Lebanon, via Iraq and Syria.

But the pipeline won't stop there.

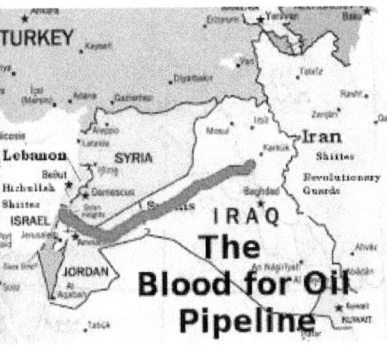

The agreement calls for the construction of an underwater pipeline under the Mediterranean Sea stretching from Lebanon to Greece to deliver Iranian gas to energy-hungry European nations.

The 6,000 kilometer pipeline, which has a massive price tag of $10 billion, will have an estimated capacity of 100-120 million cubic feet of gas per day, with a projected completion date sometime near 2018. As of this writing, the construction of this proposed pipeline has not begun and the question of who will finance the project has not been addressed. However, in July 2013, leaders from Syria, Iran, and Iraq met to sign a preliminary agreement on the pipeline with the hopes of finalizing the deal by the end of the year.

Like its Turkish neighbor, Syria's geographic location on the Mediterranean Sea makes it an obvious export center for landlocked oil producers within the greater Middle East seeking to export their oil and gas reserves to European markets. For this reason Syria's strategic location, and its warm water port on the Mediterranean, have placed it near the center of a major effort by Western nations to pump cheap Middle East gas supplies to Europe and beyond.

Syria is already part of a Western-ordained gas pipeline that spans from Egypt to Homs. This pipeline, known as the Arab Gas Pipeline, was originally planned to continue traveling north of Homs up into Turkey. From there, it can be piped into Europe. The major players of this Western approved pipeline include Saudi Arabia and Qatar, among other Gulf nations.

Syrian President Assad has since rejected the Arab Gas Pipeline and has instead begun working closely with Iran on Iran's proposed gas pipeline, dubbed the Islamic Pipeline. This proposed pipeline would obviously compete directly with the Arab Gas Pipeline and its goal of delivering Mideast natural gas to Europe.

Most Arabs view the Islamic Pipeline as a Shi'ite pipeline serving Shi'ite interests. After all, it originates in Shi'ite Iran, passes through Shi'ite Iraq, and flows into Shi'ite controlled Syria. Therefore, the Sunni-dominated Gulf nations have both an economic and to a lesser extent, a religious reason, for stopping the Islamic Pipeline from becoming a reality. So far, the Gulf nations have violently opposed Syria's adoption of the Islamic Pipeline by arming opposition fighters within Syria in order to destabilize the nation. While the ultimate goal is to topple the Assad regime, these hopes appear to be diminishing as Assad remains strong and defiant in the face of recent opposition.

Despite his firm grip on power, Syrian President Bashar Al-Assad is opposed by many powerful actors within the Middle East, including Israel, Jordan, Turkey, Qatar, and Saudi Arabia. Al Qaeda also strongly opposes the Assad government and has joined other rebel factions in an effort to overthrow Assad and to install a more Sunni-friendly (and perhaps more importantly, a Western-friendly) government.

This week, it appears that the long planned U.S.-led war in Syria may finally commence. For nearly two decades, Western nations have been plotting an overthrow of the Syrian government with the aim of replacing the hostile regime with a new "democratic" government that is friendly to Western interests in the region. The official Western narrative against Syria goes something like this:

The Syrian government has abused basic human rights, maintains deep ties with rogue regimes like Iran and North Korea, and just recently launched a chemical weapons strike on hundreds of its own people. In addition to killing its own people, the Assad regime is serving to destabilize an already unstable Middle East. Assad must go...

According to most reports, the U.S., Britain, and France are preparing for a strike against numerous key targets within Syria this week.

British Prime Minister, David Cameron, is calling for war and has recalled Parliament this week to discuss a military response against Syria.

French President, Francois Hollande, has increased its support for the Syrian rebels and has said that France is "ready to punish" whoever was responsible for the recent chemical weapons attack.

The Arab League has blamed the chemical weapons attacks on the Syrian government and is calling for United Nations intervention.

U.S. Secretary of State, John Kerry, has said that the evidence of a chemical weapons attack in Syria is "undeniable."

After providing the White House with "all options for all contingencies," U.S. Secretary of Defense, Chuck Hagel, has stated that U.S. forces are "ready" to launch a strike against Syria.

Of course, all of this is mere propaganda, as the U.S. has long planned to topple Syria.

First, consider these words from U.S. General Wesley Clark. Clark, who is clearly a globalist, admitted that the U.S. had already made the decision to invade Syria as early as 2001.

Additionally, more damning evidence of the West's intention to launch a pre-emptive strike on Syria was revealed in an explosive report released by the UK's Daily Mail on January 2013. Below is a snippet of the report, which was entitled, U.S. 'backed plan to launch chemical weapon attack on Syria and blame it on Assad's regime' :

Leaked emails have allegedly proved that the White House gave the green light to a chemical weapons attack in Syria that could be blamed on Assad's regime and in turn, spur international military action in the devastated country. A report released on Monday contains an email exchange between two senior officials at British-based contractor Britam Defence where a scheme 'approved by Washington' is outlined explaining that Qatar would fund rebel forces in Syria to use chemical weapons.

Here's the text of the email, according to the report:

'Phil... We've got a new offer. It's about Syria again. Qataris propose an attractive deal and swear that the idea is approved by Washington.

'We'll have to deliver a CW to Homs, a Soviet origin g-shell from Libya similar to those that Assad should have. They want us to deploy our Ukrainian personnel that should speak Russian and make a video record.

'Frankly, I don't think it's a good idea but the sums proposed are enormous."

MOSCOW | Wed Sep 4, 2013 1:29pm EDT

A Russian expert report shows a makeshift weapon used in a chemical attack near the Syrian city of Aleppo in March was similar to ones made by rebels, the Russian Foreign Ministry said on Wednesday.

In a statement, the ministry suggested the Russian findings were being ignored and also said that nations that blame the Syrian government for a chemical attack near Damascus last month have played down evidence to the contrary.

The Start of World War Three

Here's my take on the beginning of WW3. Obama will order the attack on Syria. Syria will respond will missiles on Israel. Israel will return missile fire on Syria. Iran will rain down missiles on Israel, and Israel will answer with missiles and aircraft. Russia will attack Israel. By this time Israel has been destroyed and World War Three is in full swing – billions of people have been killed.

And this happened because of an oil and natural gas pipeline that runs through Syria. It is the same pipeline that runs through Iraq and

Afghanistan. The Iraq war was started because of what flows through the pipeline and we invaded Afghanistan for the same reason. Now it's Syria.

Every country in the Middle East wants that pipeline, especially Saudi Arabia. The U.S. wants it, Russia and Iran want it. China wants it, but will lie back for awhile. It was never really about chemical weapons. It has always been about oil – Greyeagle.

The US Government Stands Revealed to the World as a Collection of War Criminals and Liars

Does the American public have the strength of character to face the fact that the US government stands before the entire world revealed as a collection of war criminals who lie every time that they open their mouth? Will Congress and the American public buy the White House lie that they must support war criminals and liars or "America will lose face"?

The Obama regime's lies are so transparent and blatant that the cautious, diplomatic President Putin of Russia lost his patience and stated the fact that we all already know: John Kerry is a liar. Putin said: "This was very unpleasant and surprising for me. We talk to them [the Americans], and we assume they are decent people, but he [Kerry] is lying and he knows that he is lying. This is sad."

When Secretary of State Colin Powell was sent by the criminal Bush regime to lie to the UN, Powell and his chief of staff claim that Powell did not know he was lying. It did not occur to the Secretary of State that the White House would send him to the UN to start a war that killed, maimed, and dispossessed millions of Iraqis on the basis of total lies.

The despicable John Kerry knows that he is lying. Here is the American Secretary of State, and Obama, the puppet president, knowingly lying to the world. There is not a shred of integrity in the US government. No respect for truth, justice, morality or human life. Here are two people so evil that they want to repeat in Syria what the Bush war criminals did in Iraq.

How can the American people and their representatives in Congress tolerate these extraordinary criminals? Why are not Obama and John Kerry impeached? The Obama regime has every quality of Nazi Germany and Stasi Communist Germany, only that the Obama regime is worse. The Obama regime spies on the entire world and lies about it. The Obama regime is fully engaged in killing people in seven countries, a murderous rampage that not even Hitler attempted.

Whether the criminal Obama regime can purchase the collaboration of Congress and the European puppet states in a transparent war crime will soon be decided. The decision will determine the fate of the world.

As for facts, the report released to the UN by the Russian government concludes that the weapons used in chemical attacks in Syria are similar to the weapons in the hands of al-Nusra and are different from the weapons known to be possessed by Syria.

The Obama regime has released no evidence to the UN. This is because the criminal regime has no evidence, only made up fairy tales.

If the Obama regime had any evidence, the evidence would have been released to British Prime Minister David Cameron to enable him to carry the vote of Parliament. In the absence of evidence, Cameron had to admit to Parliament that he had no evidence, only a belief that the Syrian government had used chemical weapons. Parliament told Washington's puppet that the British people were not going to war on the basis of the Prime Minister's unsubstantiated belief.

Are the American people and the rest of the world just going to stand there, sucking their thumbs, while a new Nazi State rises in Washington?

Congress must vote down the war and make it clear to Obama that if he defies the constitutional power of Congress he will be impeached.

If the US Congress is too corrupt or incompetent to do its duty, the rest of the world must join the UN General Secretary and the President of Russia and declare that unilateral military aggression by the US government is a war crime, and that the war criminal US government will be isolated in the international community. Any of its members caught traveling abroad will be arrested and turned over to the Hague for trial – Paul Craig Roberts.

Now here's something to ponder:

In a speech today at the G20 Summit in Russia, President Barack Obama stated that members of Congress should listen to their voters but ultimately should act on their own, against their constituency, in order to make a decision that is "right for America" – Greyeagle.

Something Strange Happening here; Conjures up Thoughts Galore:

Barack Obama: The Ghost of Columbia University

I just returned from New York, where I attended my 30th Columbia University reunion. I celebrated with my esteemed classmates. Everyone except Barack Obama. As usual- he wasn't there. Not even a video greeting. Not a personalized letter to his classmates. Nothing. But worse, no one at our 30th reunion ever met him. The President of the United States is the ghost of Columbia University.

I'm certainly no "Johnny come lately." For five years now (since 2007 when it became clear Barack Obama was running for President), I've been quoted in the media as saying that no one I've ever met at Columbia can remember ever meeting, or even seeing, our college classmate Barack Obama. Don't you think the media should be asking questions? Isn't this a very strange story? Wayne Root.

Why Are Obama and Kerry So Desperate to Start a New War?

What is the real agenda?

Why is the Obama Regime so desperate to commit a war crime despite the warnings delivered to the White House Fool two days ago by the most important countries in the world at the G20 Summit?

What powerful interest is pushing the White House Fool to act outside of law, outside the will of the American people, outside the warnings of the world community?

The Obama Regime has admitted, as UK Prime Minister David Cameron had to admit, that no one has any conclusive evidence that the Assad government in Syria used chemical weapons. Nevertheless, Obama has sent the despicable john Kerry out to convince the public and Congress on the basis of videos that Assad used chemical weapons "against his own people."

What the videos show are dead and suffering people. The videos do not show who did it. The Obama Regime's case is nonexistent. It rests on nothing that indicates responsibility. The Obama Regime's case is nothing but an unsubstantiated allegation.

What kind of depraved person would take the world to war based on nothing whatsoever but an unsubstantiated allegation?

The world's two worse liars, Obama and Kerry, say Assad did it, but they admit that they cannot prove it. It is what they want to believe, because they want it to be true. The lie serves their undeclared agenda.

If Obama and Kerry were to tell the public the real reasons they want to attack Syria, they would be removed from office.

The entire world is teetering on a war, the consequences of which are unknown, for no other reason than two people, devoid of all integrity who lack the intelligence and humanity to be in high office, are determined to serve a tiny collection of warmongers consisting of the crazed, murderous Israeli government and their Muslim-hating neoconservative agents, who comprise a fifth column inside the Obama Regime.

The Russian government has given evidence to the UN that conclusively proves that the al-Nusra, al-Qaeda affiliated invaders are responsible for the attack. There is also conclusive proof that the "rebels" have chemical weapons. In addition, a highly regarded journalist has reported, using direct quotes and the names of al-Nusra fighters, that the chemical weapons were given to al-Nusra by Saudi Arabia without proper handling instructions, and that an accidental explosion occurred before al-Nusra could use the Saudi-supplied weapons to frame-up the Assad government.

However the deaths were caused, they are unfortunate, but no more so that the deaths that Obama has caused in Iraq, Afghanistan, Libya, Somalia, Pakistan, Yemen, Egypt, and Syria. The proven deaths for which Obama is responsible are many times the unproven deaths that Obama attributes without evidence to Assad.

The indisputable fact is that Syrian deaths occur only because Washington initiated the invasion of Syria by external forces similar to the ones that Washington used against Libya. However the deaths occurred, the deaths are the doings of the criminal Obama Regime. Without the criminal Obama Regime seeking the overthrow of the Syrian government, there would be no deaths by chemical weapons or by any other means. This was a war initiated by Washington, Israel, Israel's neoconservative fifth column inside America and the White House, and the captive western media that is bought and paid for by the Israel Lobby.

Assad did not start the war. The Syrian government was attacked by outside forces sent in by Washington and Israel.

Assad has much higher public support in Syria than Obama has in the US, or Cameron has in the UK, or Hollande has in France, or Merkel has in Germany, or Netanyahu has in Israel.

The White House Fool keeps repeating his nonsensical statement, as if the Fool is a wound-up talking doll, and that Assad's unproven "use of chemical weapons is a threat to global security."

Dear reader, who besides the White House Fool is so unbelievably stupid as to believe that Syria is a threat to world security?

If Syria is a "threat to world security," like Iraq was a "threat to world security," like Iran is alleged to be a "threat to world security," what kind of superpower is the United States? How low does the IQ have to be, how mentally impaired does the public have to be to fall for these absurd hysterical allegations?

Let's turn Obama's claim upon the Fool. Why isn't it a threat to global security for Obama to attack Syria? There is no authority for Obama to attack Syria just because he wants to and just because he has demonized Assad with endless lies and just because Obama is the total puppet of the crazed Israeli government and his neoconservative national security advisor, in effect an Israeli agent, and just because the Ministry of Propaganda, including NPR, repeats every Obama lie as if it were the truth.

Isn't it a threat to international security when a superpower can, acting on a whim, demonize a leader and a country and unleash mass destruction, as the US has done seven times in the past twelve years,? There are millions of innocent but demonized victims of the "indispensable, exceptional USA," the "light unto the world."

Forget about the US media, which is nothing but a propaganda ministry for the Israel Lobby. What the members of Congress and what the American people need to ask Obama is why does the White House only represent the Israel Lobby?

No one supports an attack on Syria but the Israel Lobby.

Why is Obama going to add yet another war crime to Washington's 12-year record? Wasn't it enough to destroy the lives and prospects of millions of people in Afghanistan, Iraq, Libya, Somalia, Pakistan, Yemen, and Egypt?

Why kill and destroy the life prospects of yet more millions of people in Syria and other countries into which Obama's war could spread?

Maybe the answer is that Obama, Kerry, and the crazed Netanyahu and his neoconservative fifth column are zombies – Paul Craig Roberts.

CHAPTER THREE

Too Many Years Of Lies: From Mossadeq to 9/11

Washington has been at war for 12 years. According to experts such as Joseph Stiglitz and Linda Bilmes, these wars have cost Americans approximately $6 trillion, enough to keep Social Security and Medicare sound for years. All there is to show for 12 years of war is fat bank balances for the armament industries and a list of destroyed countries with millions of dead and dislocated people who never lifted a hand against the United States.

The cost paid by American troops and taxpayers is extreme. Secretary of Veteran Affairs Erik Shinseki reported in November 2009 that "more veterans have committed suicide since 2001 than we have lost on the battlefields of Iraq and Afghanistan." Many thousands of our troops have suffered amputations and traumatic brain injuries. At the Marine Corps War College Jim Lacey calculated that the annual cost of the Afghan war was $1.5 billion for each al-Qaeda member in Afghanistan. Many US and coalition troops paid with their lives for every one al-Qaeda member killed. On no basis has the war ever made sense.

Washington's wars have destroyed the favorable image of the United States created over the decades of the cold war. No longer the hope of mankind, the US today is viewed as a threat whose government cannot be trusted.

The wars that have left America's reputation in tatters are the consequence of 9/11. The neoconservatives who advocate America's hegemony over the world called for "a new Pearl Harbor" that would allow them to launch wars of conquest. Their plan for conquering the Middle East as their starting point was set out in the neoconservative "Project for the New American Century." It was stated clearly by Commentary editor Norman Podhoretz and also by many neoconservatives.

The neocon argument boils down to a claim that history has chosen "democratic capitalism" and not Karl Marx as the future. To comply with history's choice, the US must beef up its military and impose the American Way on the entire world.

In other words, as Claes Ryn wrote, the American neoconservatives are the "new Jacobins," a reference to the French Revolution of 1789 that intended to overthrow aristocratic Europe and replace it with "Liberty, equality, fraternity," but instead gave Europe a quarter century of war, death, and destruction.

Ideologies are dangerous, because they are immune to facts. Now that the United States is no longer governed by the US Constitution, but by a crazed ideology that has given rise to a domestic police state more complete than that of Communist East Germany and to a warfare state that attacks sovereign countries based on nothing but manufactured lies, we are left with the irony that Russia and China are viewed as constraints on Washington's ability to inflict evil, death, and destruction on the world.

The two pariah states of the 20th century have become the hope of mankind in the 21st century!

As Oliver Stone and Peter Kuznick prove in their book, The Untold History of the United States, the American government has never deserved its white hat reputation. Washington has been very successful in dressing up its crimes in moralistic language and hiding them in secrecy. It is only decades after events that the truth comes out.

For example, on August 19, 1953, the democratically elected government of Iran was overthrown by a coup instigated by the US government. Sixty years after the event declassified CIA documents detail how the secret CIA operation overthrew a democratic government and imposed Washington's puppet on the people of Iran.

The declassified documents could not have spelled it out any clearer: "The military coup that overthrew Mossadeq and his National Front cabinet was carried out under CIA direction as an act of U.S. foreign policy, conceived and approved at the highest levels of government.

In the 21st century Washington is attempting to repeat its 1953 feat of overthrowing the Iranian government, this time using the faux "green revolution" financed by Washington.

When that fails, Washington will rely on military action.

If 60 years is the time that must pass before Washington's crimes can be acknowledged, the US government will admit the truth about September 11, 2001 on September 11, 2061. In 2013, on this 12th anniversary of 9/11, we only have 48 years to go before Washington admits the truth. Alas, the members of the 9/11 truth movement will not still be alive to receive their vindication.

But just as it has been known for decades that Washington overthrew Mossadeq, we already know that the official story of 9/11 is hogwash.

No evidence exists that supports the government's 9/11 story. The 9/11 Commission was a political gathering run by a neoconservative White House operative. The Commission members sat and listened to the government's story and wrote it down. No investigation of any kind was made. One member of the Commission resigned, saying that the fix was in. After the report was published, both co-chairmen of the Commission and the legal counsel wrote books disassociating themselves from the report. The 9/11 Commission was "set up to fail," they wrote.

NIST's account of the structural failure of the twin towers is a computer simulation based on assumptions chosen to produce the result. NIST refuses to release its make-believe explanation for expert scrutiny. The reason is obvious. NIST's explanation of the structural failure of the towers cannot survive scrutiny.

There are many 9/11 Truth organizations whose members are high-rise architects, structural engineers, physicists, chemists and nano-chemists, military and civilian airline pilots, firemen and first responders, former prominent government officials, and 9/11 families. The evidence they have amassed overwhelms the feeble official account.

It has been proven conclusively that World Trade Center Building 7 fell at free fall which can only be achieved by controlled demolition that removes all resistance below to debris falling from above so that no time is lost in overcoming resistance from intact structures. NIST has acknowledged this fact, but has not changed its story.

In other words, still in America today official denial takes precedence over science and known undisputed facts.

On this 12th anniversary of a false flag event, it is unnecessary for me to report the voluminous evidence that conclusively proves that the official story is a lie. You can read it for yourself. It is available online. You can read what the architects and engineers have to say. You can read the scientists' reports. You can hear from the first responders who were in the WTC towers. You can read the pilots who say that the maneuvers associated with the airliner that allegedly hit the Pentagon are beyond their skills and most certainly were not performed by inexperienced pilots.

Actually, you do not need any of the expert evidence to know that the US government's story is false. As I have previously pointed out, had a few young Saudi Arabians, the alleged 9/11 hijackers, been capable of outwitting, without support from any government and intelligence service, not only the CIA and FBI, but all sixteen US intelligence services, the intelligence services of Washington's NATO allies and Israel's Mossad, the National Security Council, NORAD, the Joint Chiefs of Staff, Air Traffic Control, and defeat Airport Security four times in one hour on the same morning, the White House, Congress, and the media would have been demanding an investigation of how the National Security State could so totally fail.

Instead, the President of the United States and every government office fiercely resisted any investigation. It was only after a year of demands and rising pressure from the 9/11 families that the 9/11 Commission was created to bury the issue.

No one in government was held accountable for the astonishing failure. The national security state was defeated by a few rag tag Muslims with box cutters and a sick old man dying from renal failure while holed up in a cave in Afghanistan, and no heads rolled.

The total absence from the government for demands for an investigation of an event that is the greatest embarrassment to a "superpower" in world history is a complete give-away that 9/11was a false flag event. The government did not want any investigation, because the government's cover story cannot stand investigation.

The government could rely on the mega-media corporations in whose hands the corrupt Clinton regime concentrated the US media. By supporting rather than investigating the government's cover story, the media left the majority of Americans, who are sensitive to pressure, without any support for their doubts. Effectively, the American Ministry of Propaganda validated the government's false story.

Common everyday experiences of Americans refute the government's story. Consider, for example, self-cleaning ovens. How many American homes have them? Thirty million? More? Do you have one?

Do you know what temperature self-cleaning ovens reach? The self-cleaning cycle runs for several hours at 900 degrees Fahrenheit or 482 degrees Celsius. Does your self-cleaning oven melt at 482 degrees Celsius. No, it doesn't. Does the very thin, one-eighth inch steel soften and your oven collapse? No, it doesn't.

Keep that in mind while you read this: According to tests performed by NIST (National Institute of Standards and Technology), only 2% of the WTC steel tested by NIST reached temperatures as high as 250 degrees

Celsius, about half the temperature reached by your self-cleaning oven. Do you believe that such low temperatures on such small areas of the WTC towers caused the massive, thick, steel columns in the towers to soften and permit the collapse of the buildings? If you do, please explain why your self-cleaning oven doesn't weaken and collapse.

In Section E.5 of the Executive Summary in this NIST report http://www.nist.gov/customcf/get_pdf.cfm?pub_id=101019 it says: "A method was developed using microscopic observations of paint cracking to determine whether steel members had experienced temperatures in excess of 250 degrees C. More than 170 areas were examined . . . Only three locations had a positive result indicating that the steel and paint may have reached temperatures in excess of 250 degrees C." Analysis of steel "microstructures show no evidence of exposure to temperatures above 600 degrees C for any significant time."

In section 3.6 of the NIST report http://www.nist.gov/customcf/get_pdf.cfm?pub_id=101019 NIST states: "NIST believes that this collection of steel from the WTC towers is adequate for purposes of the investigation."

How did these truths get out? My explanation is that the NIST scientists, resentful of the threat to their jobs and future employment opportunities and chaffing under the order to produce a false report, revealed the coerced deception by including information that their political masters did not understand. By stating unequivocally the actual temperatures, NIST's scientists put the lie to the coerced report.

The melting point of steel is around 1,500 degrees C. or 2,600 degrees F. Steel can lose strength at lower temperatures, but the NIST scientists reported that only a small part of the steel was even subjected to moderate temperatures less than those obtained by the self-cleaning oven in your home.

If you need to think about this a bit more, obtain a copy of The Making of the Atomic Bomb by Richard Rhodes. Have a look at the streetcar in photo 108. The caption reads: "The Hiroshima fireball instantly raised surface temperatures within a mile of the hypocenter well above 1,000 degrees F." Is the streetcar a melted lump of steel? No, it is structurally intact, although blackened with burnt paint.

Washington would have you believe that steel that survived intact the atomic bomb would melt from low temperature, short lived, isolated office fires. What do you think of a government that believes that you are that stupid?

Who would support a government that lies every time it opens its mouth?

The three WTC buildings that were destroyed were massive heat sinks. I doubt that the limited, short-lived, low temperature fires in the buildings even warmed the massive steel structures to the touch.

Moreover, not a single steel column melted or deformed from softening. The columns were severed at specific lengths by extremely high temperature charges placed on the columns.

On this 12th anniversary of 9/11, ask yourself if you really want to believe that temperatures half those reached by your self-cleaning oven caused three massive steel structures to crumble into dust.

Then ask yourself why your government thinks you are so totally stupid as to believe such a fairy tale as your government has told you about 9/11 – Paul Craig Roberts.

It's not what it Seems:

Regardless of the recent offers of chemical weapons versus a strike, the Obama Administration wants to take over the Assad government and that can happen only with war. Controlling the Syrian government means control over the oil and natural gas pipeline that runs through Syria. This is the goal – Greyeagle.

MOSCOW —" RECENT events surrounding Syria have prompted me to speak directly to the American people and their political leaders. It is important to do so at a time of insufficient communication between our societies.

"Relations between us have passed through different stages. We stood against each other during the cold war. But we were also allies once, and defeated the Nazis together. The universal international organization — the United Nations — was then established to prevent such devastation from ever happening again.

"The United Nations' founders understood that decisions affecting war and peace should happen only by consensus, and with America's consent the veto by Security Council permanent members was enshrined in the United Nations Charter. The profound wisdom of this has underpinned the stability of international relations for decades.

"No one wants the United Nations to suffer the fate of the League of Nations, which collapsed because it lacked real leverage. This is possible if influential countries bypass the United Nations and take military action without Security Council authorization.

"The potential strike by the United States against Syria, despite strong opposition from many countries and major political and religious leaders, including the pope, will result in more innocent victims and escalation, potentially spreading the conflict far beyond Syria's borders. A strike would increase violence and unleash a new wave of terrorism. It could undermine multilateral efforts to resolve the Iranian nuclear problem and the Israeli-Palestinian conflict and further destabilize the Middle East and North Africa. It could throw the entire system of international law and order out of balance.

"Syria is not witnessing a battle for democracy, but an armed conflict between government and opposition in a multi-religious country. There are few champions of democracy in Syria. But there are more than enough Qaeda fighters and extremists of all stripes battling the government."

The United States State Department has designated Al Nusra Front and the Islamic State of Iraq and the Levant, fighting with the opposition, as terrorist organizations. This internal conflict, fueled by foreign weapons supplied to the opposition, is one of the bloodiest in the world.

Mercenaries from Arab countries fighting there, and hundreds of militants from Western countries and even Russia, are an issue of our deep concern. Might they not return to our countries with experience acquired in Syria? After all, after fighting in Libya, extremists moved on to Mali. This threatens us all.

From the outset, Russia has advocated peaceful dialogue enabling Syrians to develop a compromise plan for their own future. We are not protecting the Syrian government, but international law. We need to use the United Nations Security Council and believe that preserving law and order in today's complex and turbulent world is one of the few ways to keep international relations from sliding into chaos. The law is still the law, and we must follow it whether we like it or not. Under current international law, force is permitted only in self-defense or by the decision of the Security Council. Anything else is unacceptable under the United Nations Charter and would constitute an act of aggression.

No one doubts that poison gas was used in Syria. But there is every reason to believe it was used not by the Syrian Army, but by opposition forces, to provoke intervention by their powerful foreign patrons, who would be siding with the fundamentalists. Reports that militants are preparing another attack — this time against Israel — cannot be ignored.

It is alarming that military intervention in internal conflicts in foreign countries has become commonplace for the United States. Is it in America's long-term interest? I doubt it.

Millions around the world increasingly see America not as a model of democracy but as relying solely on brute force, cobbling coalitions together under the slogan "you're either with us or against us."

But force has proved ineffective and pointless. Afghanistan is reeling, and no one can say what will happen after international forces withdraw. Libya is divided into tribes and clans. In Iraq the civil war continues, with dozens killed each day. In the United States, many draw an analogy between Iraq and Syria, and ask why their government would want to repeat recent mistakes.

No matter how targeted the strikes or how sophisticated the weapons, civilian casualties are inevitable, including the elderly and children, whom the strikes are meant to protect.

The world reacts by asking: if you cannot count on international law, then you must find other ways to ensure your security. Thus a growing number of countries seek to acquire weapons of mass destruction. This is logical: if you have the bomb, no one will touch you. We are left with talk of the need to strengthen nonproliferation, when in reality this is being eroded.

We must stop using the language of force and return to the path of civilized diplomatic and political settlement.

A new opportunity to avoid military action has emerged in the past few days. The United States, Russia and all members of the international community must take advantage of the Syrian government's willingness to place its chemical arsenal under international control for subsequent destruction. Judging by the statements of President Obama, the United States sees this as an alternative to military action.

"I welcome the president's interest in continuing the dialogue with Russia on Syria. We must work together to keep this hope alive, as we agreed to at the Group of 8 meeting in Lough Erne in Northern Ireland in June, and steer the discussion back toward negotiations.

"If we can avoid force against Syria, this will improve the atmosphere in international affairs and strengthen mutual trust. It will be our shared success and open the door to cooperation on other critical issues.

"My working and personal relationship with President Obama is marked by growing trust. I appreciate this. I carefully studied his address to the nation on Tuesday. And I would rather disagree with a case he made on American exceptionalism, stating that the United

States' policy is "what makes America different. It's what makes us exceptional." It is extremely dangerous to encourage people to see themselves as exceptional, whatever the motivation. There are big countries and small countries, rich and poor, those with long democratic traditions and those still finding their way to democracy. Their policies differ, too. We are all different, but when we ask for the Lord's blessings, we must not forget that God created us equal."

Vladimir V. Putin is the president of Russia.

President Obama must promise not to arm rebel forces or Syrian dictator Bashar Assad will not hand over his chemical weapons, the em-preembattled leader told a Russian state media outlet today while demanding that Israel also surrender its nuclear arsenal.

"When we see that the U.S. genuinely stands for stability in our region, stops threatening us with military intervention and stops supplying terrorists with weapons, then we will consider it possible to finalize necessary procedures and they will become legitimate and acceptable for Syria," Assad told RIA News.

Obama asked Congress to postpone a vote authorizing use of military force in Syria after Russian President Vladimir Putin offered to broker a deal whereby the U.S. would not attack the Assad regime if he surrendered his chemical weapons.

Assad said that the Middle East won't have peace until Israel also surrenders its weapons of mass destruction - **JOEL GEHRKE**

Crushing Response Waiting for Any Possible US Strike on Syria:

TEHRAN (FNA)- Shanghai Daily editor Lancy Correa believes that US President Barack Obama was isolated and in the corner both at home and abroad when he was pushing for war on Syria last week and the Russian initiative has gifted him a way out, otherwise his strike order would be met with a crushing response from the side of Syria.

"It's stupid to think that Syria will sit idly by if it is attacked. President Assad has pledged retaliation and insisted that it will not back down if it is assailed militarily," Correa said during an interview with FNA.

Correa is a foreign expert and editor at Shanghai Daily. He has also been a news editor at The Nation in Bangkok, and chief sub-editor at Indian Express.

What follows is his interview with FNA on the US war on Syria, especially after the Russian proposal for international control over Syria's chemical weapons in return for the annulment of the US war plan on the crisis-hit country.

1. What do the American and the world public think of a military intervention in Syria? And why?

It's pretty obvious from all the polls that the American public and world opinion is NOT in favor of any kind of military (mis)adventure in Syria. The reasons, too, are obvious. People around the world, in general, and the American public in particular are tired of wars being raged around the world, especially in the Middle East and Asia, in their name. Amid an economic crisis that has sapped confidence the public has no appetite for any military intervention anywhere.

2. What will be the final decision of the US Congress on intervention in Syria? What do congressional and constituency offices tell us about any upcoming voting in the Senate or the House?

The Congress seems to be deeply divided over the issue and most constituents of congressmen and senators apparently have been calling them and urging them not to vote for any resolution that allows for military intervention in Syria.

3. What were the reasons that Obama devolved the decision on military attack to the Congress?

President Obama had pushed himself into a corner by suggesting a red line in case chemical weapons are used in the Syria conflict. Now that it has been "confirmed" chemical arms were used in a so-called attack last month, even though there is no absolute proof that it was President Assad who ordered it, the mere fact of its use has propelled the US to look and act tough.

4. What consequences can a military strike against Syria have in the country and the region? What will happen if the rebels take control in Syria? Will it be safer?

It's hard to say what will happen in case of military strikes in Syria since the region itself, even without any conflict, is pretty volatile with its layers of ethnic and religious sensibilities. If the rebels take control of Syria, it is likely that the country will go the way of Iraq and Libya, it will unravel and the timorous peace that has held its different people, the Alawites, Shias, Sunnis, Kurds, Christians, etc will undoubtedly be shattered. Look no further than the non-states that Iraq and Libya have become since they were invaded and the regime-change imposed on them.

5. There's a perception in the West that if Syria is attacked, Damascus and its allies will not react or respond it. Do you think that Syria and its allies naming Russia and Iran will certainly not react to this?

It's stupid to think that Syria will sit idly by if it is attacked. President Assad has pledged retaliation and insisted that it will not back down if it is assailed militarily. Its allies Russia and Iran may not join in the conflict militarily but will use their influence elsewhere to rally the world, which at least Russia has been doing very well, and consistently, since the Syrian conflict began.

6. Russia has proposed to keep Syrian chemical weapons under international control provided that the threat of military attack against Syria is removed. Damascus welcomed this initiative. What is your take on this? Will it decrease the possibility of any attack against Syria? Or the West will find another pretext to attack the country?

Apparently, the US also seems to like the idea though President Obama has been a bit skeptical. He has, however, agreed to consider it thoroughly. So it seems there is a broad agreement over the control of Syria's chemical weapons arsenal. Whether it will lead to a long-term, political solution is still to be seen, since the Syrian opposition seems to be out for blood, and I can't see them agreeing to anything short of President Assad's ouster – Lancy Correa.

U.S. Military: Al-Qaeda Rebels Produced Sarin Gas For Chemical Attacks In Syria

Further evidence that the Aug. 21 chemical attack was a false flag to frame Assad:

A leaked U.S. military document reveals that Al-Qaeda possessed and produced "kitchen-grade" sarin gas for chemical attacks against the Syrian people, further adding to the evidence that the Al-Qaeda Syrian opposition launched the Aug. 21 chemical attack in Damascus as a false flag in order to frame Syrian President Bashar Al-Assad.

In May, Turkish anti-terror police confiscated a two-kilogram cylinder of sarin gas from members of the Jabhat al-Nusra Front based in Southern Turkey near the Syrian border, according to a classified report obtained by WND.

The National Ground Intelligence Center report states that Al-Qaeda in Iraq produced the sarin gas and then shipped it to the al-Nusra Front for use in Syria.

Two months prior to the confiscation, 26 people and Syrian government forces died from exposure to sarin gas delivered in a rocket attack on Aleppo, a city in the northwestern region of Syria near the Turkish border.

"The rocket came from a place controlled by the terrorists and which is located close to the Turkish territory," according to a Syrian government statement in response to the attack. "One can assume that the weapon came from Turkey."

The document also describes the sarin seized in Turkey as not being military grade but rather a "kitchen variety," which corresponds to the sarin gas used in the Aug. 21 chemical attack near Damascus, according to Dr. Yossef Bodansky, a top terrorism expert.

Bodansky said that unlike military grade sarin, the sarin used in the Damascus attack did not accumulate around the victims' hair and clothing.

If it did, said Bodansky, the sarin molecules would have detached from the victims and "killed or injured the first responders who touched the victims' bodies without protective clothes ... and masks."

Yet there were no reported casualties among the first responders to the attack, none of whom were wearing adequate protective gear.

High-level U.S. intelligence officials reinforce Bodansky's conclusion, stating that they are not convinced that the Aug. 21 chemical attack was carried out per Assad's orders or that it was even carried out by Assad's government.

They are not even sure that Assad knew about the attack beforehand.

Intercepted Syrian military communications reveal that after the Aug. 21 attack, the Syrian general staff were in a complete panic thinking that their 155th Brigade launched an unauthorized chemical strike in defiance of prior orders not to do so.

This led to Syrian intelligence interrogating the major in charge of the brigade for three days, who adamantly denied firing any missiles and encouraged the general staff to count his weapons inventory.

All of the brigade's missiles were accounted for.

Pierre Piccinin da Prata, a Belgium writer who was kidnapped by the al-Nursa Front, said that during his captivity he overheard his rebel captors admit that they carried out the Aug. 21 chemical attack as a false flag in order to lure the United States into the conflict to help Al-Qaeda topple Assad.

"The government of Bashar al-Assad did not use sarin gas or other types of gas in the outskirts of Damascus," Piccinin said during an interview with a Belgium radio station.

Secluded from the outside world after being kidnapped, he only learned about the attack straight from his captors.

While the Obama administration continues to push our military into entering Syria as "al-Qaeda's air force," fighting alongside Islamic extremists recruited and armed by the CIA, the evidence strongly points to the al-Nusra Front, designated by the U.S. as a terrorist organization, as responsible for the Aug. 21 chemical attack – Kit Daniels.

Putin Steps Into World Leadership Role

Putin's article in the September 11 New York Times has the stuck pigs squealing. The squealing stuck pigs are just who you thought they would be—all those whose agendas and profits would be furthered by an attack on Syria by the Obama Stasi regime.

Included among the squealing stuck pigs are Human Rights Watch bloggers who seem to be financed out of the CIA's back pocket.

Does any institution remain that has not been corrupted by Washington's money?

Notice that the reason Putin is being criticized is that he has blocked the Obama regime from attacking Syria and slaughtering countless numbers of Syrians in the name of human rights. The stuck pigs are outraged that Obama's war has been blocked. They were so much looking forward to the mass slaughter that they believe would advance their profits and agendas.

Most of Putin's critics are too intellectually challenged to comprehend that Putin's brilliant and humane article has left Putin the leader of the free world and defender of the rule of law and exposed Obama for what he is—the leader of a rogue, lawless, unaccountable government committed to lies and war crimes.

Putin, being diplomatic, was very careful in his criticism of Obama's September 10 speech in which Obama sought to justify Washington's lawlessness in terms of "American exceptionalism." Obama, attempting to lift his criminal regime by the bootstraps up into the moral heavens, claimed that United States government policy is "what makes America different. It's what makes us exceptional."

What Obama told Americans is exactly what Hitler told the Germans. The Russians, having borne more than anyone else the full weight of the German war machine, know how dangerous it is to encourage people to think of themselves as exceptional, unbound by law, the Geneva Conventions, the UN Security Council, and humane concerns for others. Putin reminded Obama that "God created us equal."

If Putin had wanted to give Obama the full rebuke that Obama deserves, Putin could have said: "Obama is correct that the policy of the US government is what makes the US exceptional. The US is the only country in the world that has attacked 8 countries in 12 years, murdering and dispossessing millions of Muslims all on the basis of lies. This is not an exceptionalism of which to be proud."

Putin is obviously more than a match for the immoral, low grade morons that Americans put into high office. However, Putin should not underestimate the mendacity of his enemies in Washington. Putin warned that the militants that Washington is breeding in the Middle East are an issue of deep concern.

When these militants return to their own countries, they spread destabilization, as when extremists used by the US in the overthrow of Libya moved on to Mali.

The destabilization of other countries is precisely the main aim of Washington's wars in the Middle East. Washington intends for radicalization of Muslims to spread strife into the Muslim populations of Russia and China. Washington's propaganda machine will then turn these terrorists into "freedom fighters against oppressive Russian and Chinese governments," and use Human Rights Watch and other organizations that Washington has penetrated and corrupted to denounce Russia and China for committing war crimes against freedom fighters. No doubt, chemical weapons attacks will be orchestrated, just as they have been in Syria.

If Washington's NATO puppet states wake up in time, the warmongers in Washington can be isolated, and humanity could be spared WWIII – Paul Craig Roberts.

24 Fast Facts About The Federal Reserve – Please Share With Everyone You Know

As we approach the 100 year anniversary of the creation of the Federal Reserve, it is absolutely imperative that we get the American people to understand that the Fed is at the very heart of our economic problems. It is a system of money that was created by the bankers and that operates for the benefit of the bankers.

The American people like to think that we have a "democratic system", but there is nothing "democratic" about the Federal Reserve.

Unelected, unaccountable central planners from a private

central bank run our financial system and manage our economy. There is a reason why financial markets respond with a yawn when Barack Obama says something about the economy, but they swing wildly whenever Federal Reserve Chairman Ben Bernanke opens his mouth. The Federal really works, they would be screaming for it to be abolished immediately. The following are 25 fast facts about the Federal Reserve that everyone should know... Reserve has far more power over the U.S. economy than anyone else does by a huge margin. The Fed is the biggest Ponzi scheme in the history of the world, and if the American people truly understood how it

The greatest period of economic growth in U.S. history was when there was no central bank.

The United States never had a persistent, ongoing problem with inflation until the Federal Reserve was created. In the century before the Federal Reserve was created, the average annual rate of inflation was about half a percent. In the century since the Federal Reserve was created, the average annual rate of inflation has been about 3.5 percent, and it would be even higher than that if the inflation numbers were not being so grossly manipulated.

Even using the official numbers, the value of the U.S. dollar has declined by more than 95 percent since the Federal Reserve was created nearly 100 years ago.

The secret November 1910 gathering at Jekyll Island, Georgia during which the plan for the Federal Reserve was hatched was attended by U.S. Senator Nelson W. Aldrich, Assistant Secretary of the Treasury Department A.P. Andrews and a whole host of representatives from the upper crust of the Wall Street banking establishment.

The following comes directly from the Fed's official mission statement: "To provide the nation with a safer, more flexible, and more stable monetary and financial system. Over the years, its role in banking and the economy has expanded."

It was not an accident that a permanent income tax was also introduced the same year when the Federal Reserve system was established. The whole idea was to transfer wealth from our pockets to the federal government and from the federal government to the bankers.

Within 20 years of the creation of the Federal Reserve, the U.S. economy was plunged into the Great Depression.

If you can believe it, there have been 10 different economic recessions since 1950. The Federal Reserve created the "dotcom bubble", the Federal Reserve created the "housing bubble" and now it has created the largest bond bubble in the history of the planet.

According to an official government report, the Federal Reserve made 16.1 trillion dollars in secret loans to the big banks during the last financial crisis. The following is a list of loan recipients that was taken directly from page 131 of the report...

Citigroup – **$2.513 trillion**
Morgan Stanley – **$2.041 trillion**
Merrill Lynch – **$1.949 trillion**
Bank of America – **$1.344 trillion**
Barclays PLC – **$868 billion**
Bear Sterns – **$853 billion**
Goldman Sachs – **$814 billion**
Royal Bank of Scotland – **$541 billion**
JP Morgan Chase – **$391 billion**
Deutsche Bank – **$354 billion**
UBS – **$287 billion**
Credit Suisse – **$262 billion**
Lehman Brothers – **$183 billion**
Bank of Scotland – **$181 billion**
BNP Paribas – **$175 billion**
Wells Fargo – **$159 billion**
Dexia – **$159 billion**
Wachovia – **$142 billion**

Dresdner Bank – **$135 billion**
Societe Generale – **$124 billion**
"All Other Borrowers" – **$2.639 trillion**

The Federal Reserve also paid those big banks $659.4 million in fees to help "administer" those secret loans.

The Federal Reserve has created approximately 2.75 trillion dollars out of thin air and injected it into the financial system over the past five years. This has allowed the stock market to soar to unprecedented heights, but it has also caused our financial system to become extremely unstable.

We were told that the purpose of quantitative easing is to help "stimulate the economy", but today the Federal Reserve is actually paying the big banks not to lend out 1.8 trillion dollars in "excess reserves" that they have parked at the Fed.

Quantitative easing overwhelming benefits those that own stocks and other financial investments. In other words, quantitative easing overwhelmingly favors the very wealthy. Even Barack Obama has admitted that 95 percent of the income gains since he has been president have gone to the top one percent of income earners.

#15 The gap between the top one percent and the rest of the country is now the greatest that it has been since the 1920s.

The Federal Reserve has argued vehemently in federal court that it is "not an agency" of the federal government and therefore not subject to the Freedom of Information Act.

The Federal Reserve openly admits that the 12 regional Federal Reserve banks are organized "much like private corporations".

The regional Federal Reserve banks issue shares of stock to the "member banks" that own them.

The Federal Reserve system greatly favors the biggest banks. Back in 1970, the five largest U.S. banks held 17 percent of all U.S. banking industry assets. Today, the five largest U.S. banks hold <u>52 percent</u> of all U.S. banking industry assets.

The Federal Reserve is supposed to "regulate" the big banks, but it has done nothing to stop <u>a 441 trillion dollar interest rate derivatives bubble</u> from inflating which could absolutely devastate our entire financial system.

The Federal Reserve was designed to be <u>a perpetual debt machine</u>. The bankers that designed it intended to trap the U.S. government in a perpetual debt spiral from which it could never possibly escape. Since the Federal Reserve was established nearly 100 years ago, the U.S. national debt has gotten more than 5000 times larger.

The U.S. government will spend <u>more than 400 billion dollars</u> just on interest on the national debt this year.

If the average rate of interest on U.S. government debt rises to just 6 percent (and it has been much higher than that in the past), we will be paying out more than a trillion dollars a year just in interest on the national debt.

According to <u>Article I, Section 8 of the U.S. Constitution</u>, the U.S. Congress is the one that is supposed to have the authority to "coin Money, regulate the Value thereof, and of foreign Coin, and fix the Standard of Weights and Measures". So exactly why is the Federal Reserve doing it?

There are plenty of possible alternative financial systems, but at this point <u>all 187 nations</u> that belong to the IMF have a central bank. Are we supposed to believe that this is just some sort of a bizarre coincidence? – Michael Snyder.

I' Is for 'Impeachment' of the US President

TEHRAN (FNA)- The disastrous reality TV style bungle in which the White House led the nation to the brink of war without the consent of the legislature and the American people should be and is raising questions about the competency of the president of the United States.

Bombing a country with which the United States is not at war in a situation in which no treaties either with the United Nations or NATO provide even a minimal fig leaf of legal cover has been described by the administration as a critical humanitarian mission even though it would not change facts on the ground in Syria and would only succeed in killing more civilians. But proceeding beyond that prodigious logical disconnect, there should also be some questions about the general deportment of the White House in terms of how its foreign policy enhances the liberties and broader interests of the American people. Has this administration made the world a safer place for American travelers and businessmen while upholding the rule of law and supporting and defending the Constitution of the United States? Or, does Barack Obama, eulogized by his admirers as a constitutional lawyer of some distinction, adhere to the sentiments of his predecessor in office, who believed in absolute executive authority and described the Constitution as just a piece of paper?

The "piece of paper" is deliberately vague regarding impeachment. Article II section 4 of the Constitution states "The President, Vice President and all civil Officers of the United States, shall be removed from Office on Impeachment for, and Conviction of, Treason, Bribery, or other high Crimes and Misdemeanors." President Obama has not been accused of taking bribes unless one considers the modalities of modern campaign finance to be a form of bribery. But Article III section 3 of the Constitution includes "Treason against the United States, shall consist only in levying War against them, or in adhering to their Enemies, giving the Aid and Comfort." By that standard and based on the 2013 Authorization for the Use of Military Force (AUMF), which defines al-Qaeda and associated groups as the enemies of the United States, the president's both facilitating the transfer of and giving arms to rebel groups in Syria that include al-Qaeda affiliates might reasonably be considered treasonous.

And there is also the flexible question of high crimes and misdemeanors, which has historically been interpreted as being anything that the House of Representatives believes to be serious enough to fall in that category. To impeach the House must first pass by simple majority articles of impeachment, which constitute the formal allegations of malfeasance. Upon passage, the defendant is considered to be "impeached". Next, the Senate tries the accused with the Chief Justice of the United States presiding. To convict a two-thirds majority of senators is required, a measure designed to avoid frivolous impeachment actions motivated by political divisions. Conviction removes the defendant from office but there are no additional penalties.

Two presidents have been impeached and a third president, Richard Nixon, resigned before he could be charged. Andrew Johnson was tried in 1868 after he replaced his Secretary of War Edwin Stanton. Stanton's position had been guaranteed by Congressional passage of the Tenure of Office Act of 1867, which was engineered by radical republicans to keep the hard liner Stanton in place to resist reconstruction policies being introduced by the more moderate Johnson. Johnson survived the process by one vote.

Nixon's illegal activity in 1972 has been referred to as the Watergate scandal. He used government tax, law enforcement, and intelligence agencies to dig up "dirt" on his political opponents, culminating in an attempted break-in at the Democratic Party Headquarters at the Watergate complex carried out by a number of former government officials.

Bill Clinton was impeached in 1998-9 over perjury and obstruction of justice, both relating to his false testimony to an independent counsel regarding his relationship with intern Monica Lewinsky. His trial in the senate did not result in the necessary two thirds majority to convict.

Avoiding the broader issue of whether any use of American armed forces without a constitutionally mandated declaration of war should be permitted at all, is going to war against a country that does not imminently threaten the United States without any congressional approval grounds for impeachment? Particularly if the intelligence to justify such an action might well be deliberately misleading or even fabricated? Well, current Vice President Joe Biden seems to think so. In 2007 he threatened impeachment if George W. Bush attacked Iran without going to congress. But Biden is now silent on the subject and current Secretary of State John Kerry has said that President Obama can attack Syria with or without congressional approval. Fifteen congressmen are now on record as agreeing with Biden-before-he-became Vice President and have stated their belief that impeachment would be warranted if Obama were to attack Syria without asking congress, considering such an action a "high crime and misdemeanor" under Article II.

Beyond what is legal or illegal in the United States, the Nuremberg Trials of 1946, which convicted a number of Nazi leaders, clearly defined the starting of a war of aggression as the "supreme international crime," a view that was endorsed by the court's American prosecutor Robert Jackson and which was also accepted by the administration of President Harry Truman. So by that standard bombing Syria would be a war crime and President Obama would be a war criminal.

As Obama has not yet started bombing Syria, the constitutional and legal issues are somewhat moot, though I would point out that there are a number of other policies that might be examined to make a case against the president. It is now known that the Obama Administration has maintained a "kill list" for assassinating US citizens who are considered to be a threat.

The only due process the targets on the list receive is a review of their status by the White House based on secret evidence and they can be killed even if they are not in flagrante engaged in an act of terror directed against the United States. Anwar al-Awlaki was assassinated while traveling in a car in Yemen together with another American citizen and his sixteen year old son was executed two weeks later together with a number of friends while eating in a restaurant. He was allegedly not targeted by the White House but was killed due to poor intelligence. There are reportedly four more names of Americans on the list. Executing citizens without a trial and allowing no opportunity to mount a defense, an act characteristic of a police state, violates the Fifth Amendment to the Constitution which says that no one can be "deprived of life, liberty, or property without due process of law..." and the Sixth Amendment which guarantees the right to a "speedy and public trial by an impartial jury" with the right to confront the "witness against him."

The clandestine use of drones to attack and kill suspected militants in countries with which the United States is not at war has been justified by the Authorization to Use Military Force provisions of the Defense Appropriation Act. The AUMF permits the government to go after and kill members of al-Qaeda and "associated groups." Taken together with the criminalization of "material support of terrorism," nearly everyone who objects to administration counter-terror policies might well be considered a target. The AUMF also implicitly identifies the entire world, including the United States and U.S. citizens, as the part of the potential battlefield. This is a violation of Article II of the Constitution, which delegates to Congress the authority to declare war and also of the Fifth and Sixth Amendments regarding due process.

The National Security Agency's illegal spying on American citizens has been since 9/11 but it has increased dramatically under President Obama. Reviews of procedures and court cases have determined that the collection of information deviates considerably from the actual targeting of potential terrorists and exceeds the existing legal authorities that have been granted to NSA. An Edward Snowden leaked document has also recently revealed that Obama approved that the information being collected by NSA on American citizens be shared with Israel, which presumably is using the intelligence for its own purposes, possibly to target Americans, making the NSA and White House accomplices of Israeli intelligence. Spying on American citizens when there is no probable cause to do so is a violation of the Fourth Amendment, which says "The right of the people to be secure in their persons, houses, papers, and effects against unreasonable searches and seizures shall not be violated." That the United States government is sharing such information with an untrustworthy foreign government is not only illegal, it is unconscionable.

The United States under President Obama continues to operate offshore prisons, most notably at Guantanamo Bay, without any due process to permit detainees to confront the evidence against them and prove their innocence. This is a serious breach of international law normally within the purview of the International Criminal Court in The Hague, but the United States has characteristically refused to participate or endorse the actions of that body. The forced feeding of prisoners at Guantanamo is, moreover, generally considered to be torture. The United States has signed the United Nations Convention against Torture, which requires signatories to take legal action against both torturers and the government officials who order the torture to be carried out.

But no one in the federal government has been punished for torture, either at Guantanamo or in the secret CIA prisons under George W. Bush, and Attorney General Eric Holder has stated his intention to take no further action, making the United States an enabler of and participant in what most of the world regards as war crimes.

Finally, if you wish to challenge any of the above through the judicial system, you might run into a sympathetic judge, but normally you will be stonewalled. The Obama use of the state secrets privilege to have cases dismissed before going to trial far exceeds in frequency similar interference in the judicial process by George W. Bush. The privilege was created to prevent the exposure of highly sensitive information but in practice it is used to derail any challenges to malfeasance by the government. When invoking the privilege, government lawyers only have to assert that sensitive information will be revealed. The judge normally agrees and dismisses the case. Article III Section 2 of the

Constitution states that "The Trial of all Crimes...shall be by jury..." It does not allow for the dismissal of criminal charges through the state secrets privilege.

So are the Obama accomplishments worth impeachment? They go far beyond the precedents of a president firing a government minister or even lying about a sexual affair and some might even consider that they exceed the Nixon gold standard of using government resources against the political opposition. Arming terrorists while asserting the right to go to war without constitutional process; targeting and killing citizens; declaring a state of war worldwide using robot death machines; spying on citizens and sharing the information with foreign governments; running secret prisons where suspects are tortured, never tried, and never can get out; and using the judiciary to block challenges to whatever is going on is quite a record. Not exactly something to be proud of, is it?

By Philip Giraldi

Obama and Thugs Pulled Off the Heist of the Century

Wayne Allyn Root

Wayne Allyn Root is a former Libertarian Vice Presidential nominee, successful entrepreneur, small business defender, business speaker, Capital Evangelist, and media personality- appearing on over 5000 interviews in the past 5 years. Wayne's latest book is: The Ultimate Obama Survival Guide: How to Survive, Thrive, and Prosper During Obamageddon. It hit #1 in bookstores, and is currently the 6th bestselling political hardcover in America for the past year. Wayne's web site: ROOTforAmerica.com.

It is increasingly clear that the 2012 elections, both presidential and senate, were stolen by Obama, the Democratic Party, the IRS, and government employee unions. It's right out of a mob movie like "The Godfather."

The Obama Crime Family could give the mob lessons. Don Obama plays for keeps. The Don gets what he wants and when he found himself in danger of losing his power and control, Obama went to his enforcers – the IRS.

In a story reminiscent of the mob fixing union elections, the IRS enforcers conspired to destroy Don Obama's main competition – the Tea Parties and other conservative fundraising groups.

Lois Lerner was only one of many IRS big shots in DC who gave orders to IRS offices across the U.S. to "kill" the Tea Parties and other conservative groups. Their goal – steal the election. As if only days ago, the "fall gal" retired from the IRS. We can only guess what kind of massive payoff she received from Obama's donors.

The 2010 elections were the biggest embarrassment suffered by a U.S. President in modern history. The power, energy and passion of the Tea Party won the GOP an amazing 63 House seats, six Senate seats, six Governorships, and 680 seats in state legislatures. It was an historic landslide. Obama's entire agenda was threatened.

Yet, the mainstream media expects us to believe that only two years later (2012) that Tea Party energy and passion was gone...overnight. Or, perhaps they changed back to fans of Obama and the Democratic Party. What a fairytale.

The real story is that the Obama administration ordered the IRS to delay, distract, hound, harass, and intimidate Tea Party groups across the U.S. Without IRS attacks and interference, Tea Parties would have had the same influence and momentum as 2010 – when their raging energy and passion led to a shocking landslide defeat for Obama and his allies.

There is no need to question or debate any longer. We now have emails from IRS officials stating exactly that – the Tea Parties had to be stopped if Democrats wanted to win the election.

And, conservative donations had to be stalled if Democrats wanted to retain control of the U.S. Senate.

Instead of massive Tea Party rallies and record-setting fundraising for conservative candidates, Tea Party groups were busy being distracted, hounded, harassed, and intimidated by the IRS. They were busy being asked about the names of their members, names of their speakers, content of their Facebook posts, and even the content of their prayers.

Conservative media personalities (like yours truly) were attacked with IRS audits, as were Pro-Life, Pro-Israel, and Pro-Constitution groups. The tax-deductible status of Tea Party groups was purposely stalled so they could not raise money for the 2012 election.

What the biased liberal mainstream media refuses to do is connect the dots. None have the courage to state that "the fix" was in. That a fraud perpetrated by government employees handed control of the United States of America to Obama, a politician who supports government employees and their unions.

What did the IRS get out of this? The answer is pure bribery. Republicans, and especially Tea Parties, believe in limited government, smaller budgets, fewer government employees, and cutting bloated salaries, obscene pensions, and early retirement for government employees. Another Tea Party landslide would have threatened the power of government employee unions. Many government employees would have been laid off.

Does anyone believe it a coincidence that Obama met with IRS union boss Colleen Kelley at the White House the day before the targeting of Tea Parties by the IRS began? If you do, I have a bridge to sell you in Brooklyn.

Barack Obama was fraudulently re-elected. Our country was hijacked by government employees protecting their cushy lifetime jobs, bloated salaries, obscene pensions, and powerful unions.

Think I'm wrong? Evidently IRS officials don't. Several of them have been busy hiring famous and expensive law firms to defend themselves.

Where are they getting the money? Is Obama arranging for big Democratic donors like George Soros, or union political funds, to pay their legal bills? Is Obama scared to death of what these IRS bosses will say under oath? Could their testimony end his Presidency and destroy his legacy?

In the end it's clear to anyone who hasn't been brainwashed by government schools or bribed by government checks that the 2012 election was fraudulently stolen by Barack Obama.

What did Obama, Democrats, and the IRS gain?

1. The right to continue to loot the treasury with bailouts, stimulus, corporate welfare, and government contracts to his friends, donors, loyal media lackeys, and corrupt union bosses.

2. The right to continue to redistribute income from the business owners (who vote Republican) to Obama's voters (the poor, unions, and government employees).

3. The ability to save Obamacare and unionize 15 million healthcare workers – thereby raising $15 billion in union dues to elect Democrats. And of course to overwhelm middle class families with $20,000 annual health insurance bills they can't pay, thereby addicting them to government handouts.

4. The IRS itself gains tremendously. They are now in charge of policing Obamacare – a huge, new bureaucracy. It also adds thousands of new IRS agents, thereby greatly enriching the IRS union.

5. The opportunity to pass immigration amnesty, thereby producing 10 to 20 million new loyal Democratic voters.

6. The opportunity to bankrupt business owners and permanently weaken the private sector, thereby drying up donations for conservative candidates and causes.

7. The opportunity to weaken American influence internationally (see Egypt, Libya, Syria).

Obama's re-election also means he may serve long enough to appoint one or two more Supreme Court justices, whose radical leftist views will ensure America is permanently transformed to a big government socialist nation.

This wasn't just any theft, folks. It was a trillion dollar theft. The Obama Crime Family (so far) has gotten away with the greatest and most daring act of fraud in world history. They stole the election.

 Why would the president of the United States try to purposely hurt the American people? Well, in 2013 this is done in order to score political points and force the opposition in to doing what you want them to do.

A few days ago, an angry Park Service ranger publicly admitted that he and his fellow rangers have been ordered to "make life as difficult for people as we can" during this government shutdown. That Park Service ranger would never have received such an order unless it came from the very top.

Apparently the Obama administration plans to cause as much pain as possible until Obama gets everything that he is demanding. In many cases, it is actually going to cost far more money to put up barricades and use guards to keep Americans from visiting open air memorials, driving on roads, and fishing in bodies of water than it would to put up a "closed" sign and simply go home.

As you will see from the examples posted below, the Obama administration is being extremely spiteful and vindictive. And the level of hypocrisy that we are now witnessing is hard to fathom. For instance, the National Mall has been totally closed to the public, but the Obama administration is specifically reopening it for a massive pro-immigration rally that will benefit the Democrats politically. The abuse of power that is taking place is absolutely staggering, and the American people need to demand that those that are abusing it be held accountable when all of this is over.

The following are just a few examples of how Obama is using this shutdown to make life as difficult for people as possible...

#1 The Obama administration is doing all it can to keep Americans from even getting a glimpse of Mount Rushmore, but Barack Obama's chefs have been deemed "essential" and are still preparing his meals.

#2 Small businesses cannot get loans, but the exclusive gyms that are only for members of Congress have been deemed "essential" and remain open.

#3 The National Mall has been closed to the public, but it will be opened for a huge pro-immigration rally being held by Obama supporters.

#4 Last chance cancer treatments for children with cancer have been suspended, but the IRS continues to collect taxes from us.

#5 The NIH has stopped therapy dogs from visiting sick children, but Obama and Congress are still getting paid.

#6 The USDA website has been shut down, but Michelle Obama's Let's Move website is still operating.

#7 A runner has been fined $100 for jogging through Valley Forge National Historical Park, but the military golf course that Obama uses regularly is still open.

#8 The Obama administration has shut down the Grand Canyon, but the new two billion dollar NSA spy center is still spying on all of us.

#9 The federal government has forced an elderly couple out of their home on Lake Mead during this shutdown, but the operations of the Federal Reserve have not been affected at all.

#10 In South Carolina, the Obama administration is actually using Park Service rangers to keep people away from a privately-owned hotel.

#11 In Tennessee, the feds have totally shut down the Foothills Parkway, a major thoroughfare that runs through Blount County. At this point the feds are not even letting people visit the graves of their dead relatives.

#12 The Obama administration has actually removed all of the well pumps along a 184 mile trail that goes from Washington D.C. to Pittsburgh just so that anyone that decides to use the trail will not be able to get any water to drink.

#13 The Obama administration is actually attempting to close 1,100 square miles of ocean off of the coast of Florida. It is going to take a tremendous amount of time, money and energy to keep fishing boats out of that area.

#14 According to one news report, "Gestapo tactics" were used against one tour group made up mostly of senior citizens at Yellowstone National Park...

Pat Vaillancourt went on a trip last week that was intended to showcase some of America's greatest treasures.

Instead, the Salisbury resident said she and others on her tour bus witnessed an ugly spectacle that made her embarrassed, angry and heartbroken for her country.

Vaillancourt was one of thousands of people who found themselves in a national park as the federal government shutdown went into effect on Oct. 1. For many hours her tour group, which included senior citizen visitors from Japan, Australia, Canada and the United States, were locked in a Yellowstone National Park hotel under armed guard.

The tourists were treated harshly by armed park employees, she said, so much so that some of the foreign tourists with limited English skills thought they were under arrest.

When finally allowed to leave, the bus was not allowed to halt at all along the 2.5-hour trip out of the park, not even to stop at private bathrooms that were open along the route.

#15 Of course one of the most disturbing abuses of power is how the Obama administration is using barricades and guards to keep military veterans away from open air memorials such as the World War II Memorial, the Vietnam War Memorial and the Iwo Jima Memorial that are normally open to the public 24 hours a day.

It is beyond disgusting for Barack Obama to take these memorials hostage for political gain.

And a lot of military veterans have decided that they are not going to take this slap in the face. In fact, one group is organizing a "Million Veteran March on the Memorials" this weekend. You can find their Facebook page. According to their page, a mass protest is being planned for 9 AM this Sunday morning...

"Join fellow Veterans at the war memorials in Washington DC on Sunday October 13th at 9 AM and at memorials across these United States."

And veterans will not be the only ones in D.C. this weekend. An organization known as "Truckers Ride for the Constitution" will also be there. The truckers are planning a three day strike and protest which will stretch from Friday to Sunday...

"The American people are sick and tired of the corruption that is destroying America! We therefore declare a national protest in support of our nation's truckers on the weekend of October 11-13, 2013! Truck drivers will not haul freight! Americans can strike in solidarity with truck drivers! Truckers will lead the path to saving our country if every American rides with them!"

Many truckers are even planning to take their trucks right into the heart of Washington D.C. itself.

It will certainly be interesting to see what happens.

Personally, I have never seen anything like what we are witnessing right now. The president of the United States is actually trying to purposely hurt the American people in order to put pressure on Congress. He isn't even being subtle about it.

Whether you are a Democrat, a Republican or an Independent, you have got to be absolutely disgusted by what Obama is doing. He is showing an astounding lack of respect for the American people.

It is one thing to play hardball with Congress. That is acceptable. It is quite another thing to spitefully abuse the American people in order to get what you want.

What Obama has done goes way over the line. If the American people are not outraged by this, what will it take to wake them up?

Obama Kidnapped America

Wayne Allyn Root

Do you ever get the feeling our country has been stolen? Where's America? I want my country back. I think it may be time to call the police and issue an "Amber Alert." The kidnapper's name is Barack Obama. You might know him. He lives in the White House.

In the past, I've written about all the strange priorities of Obama. Priorities that suggest he's out to hurt us, not help us. But the news that Obama allowed the <u>shutdown of the "Amber Alert"</u> website certainly takes the cake.

Oh, it's back up now, after a <u>huge public outcry</u>. But as my father used to say, "Watch what a guy does, not what he says." The original action tells you all you need to know about our President. He is a man intent on hurting, damaging, or destroying middle class America, our military, our economy, and our values.

Let's start with a few actions that happened long *before* the government shutdown. Obama shut down White House tours. He released illegal alien felons from prison. He closed pools on military bases – thereby hurting the kids of our heroes away at war, defending America. He cancelled July 4th fireworks displays at military bases. He cancelled Top Gun flight training school for our best Navy fighter pilots. He cancelled "flyovers" at graduation ceremonies for our Annapolis, West Point, and Air Force Academy grads.

Is this normal behavior for a patriot? Why not cut welfare, food stamps, and stimulus spending? Why not cut "earned income tax credits" for illegal immigrants who never paid taxes in the first place? Why not cut spending on the advertising campaign in Mexico that "educates" Mexicans that their relatives in America qualify for food stamps?

Why not dramatically cut the 22 million government employees? Why not cut the obscene $100,000 and $200,000 pensions for government employees? Why not cut the foreign aid for people that hate America – like Egypt, Libya or the Palestinians?

Obama has money for all of this, but not for the military, or Amber Alerts.

We need to issue an Amber Alert. Our country has been stolen.

Who would make choices like this? Who would want to intentionally hurt members of the military, but keep spending on advertising to encourage dependence on government?

It sure feels like these are the decisions of someone who doesn't like America, who dislikes the military, and wants to make patriotic middle class Americans feel as much pain as possible.

We need to issue an Amber Alert. Our country has been stolen.

While the military and their families go without, there's plenty of money for Obama to play golf, take vacations, and spend $100 million traveling to Africa. While he was in Africa waving to adoring crowds, he pledged $7 billion to increase electricity access for Africans. With American taxpayer money? These are just not normal decisions made in the best interests of America.

We need to issue an Amber Alert. Our country has been stolen.

But the decisions Obama has made during this government shutdown take the cake. First, he tried to close down the World War II Memorial in Washington – an outdoors memorial that requires no government employee oversight in the first place. The objective? To deny entrance for 90-year-old military vets flying into Washington, D.C. for the trip of a lifetime to honor their dead comrades.

Then it was the cancellation of the broadcasting of NFL games to overseas military. Then military chaplains were threatened with arrest if they chose to work for free.

Once again, Obama shows his true colors- his disrespect for the military, veterans, and religion.

We need to issue an Amber Alert. Our country has been stolen.

Then there's the closing of national parks and recreation areas. Even privately managed parks have been shut down. Obama even shut down the ocean – fishing boat charters are prohibited from going out to sea.

However it is important to note, Obama's military golf course at Andrews Air Force Base just happens to be unaffected by the shutdown. Golf must now be deemed "an essential government service" by Obama. Maybe Obama is hunting for terrorists in golf holes?

By the way, even though Obama's home golf course remains open, the grocery stores on the base have been shut down – forcing military families to pay 30 percent more at area supermarkets. A military family eating must not be "essential" to Obama.

But all that pales in comparison to risking the entire U.S. economy on a mission to embarrass the GOP. Obama runs around the country loudly threatening a Treasury debt default, and promising "catastrophic losses," thereby inciting fear and panic among bond and stock investors across the globe. He knows this kind of talk could lead to a collapse. But that's not a concern to our President. Because he's betting that a stock crash, or economic collapse would frighten Republicans into accepting Obama's budget and re-opening the government. The President of the United States is trying to incite a financial crash. Isn't that called terrorism?

We need to issue an Amber Alert. Our country has been stolen.

What matters to Obama is to purposely inflict as much damage as possible, as long as the Republican Party is destroyed. As Obama's hero Saul Alinsky said, "the end justifies the means." Alinsky's end was the destruction of capitalism and America.

Obama is quite simply the biggest bully ever in the White House. He uses exaggeration, extortion, fraud and intimidation to attack his opponents and get his way. The Obama Crime Family makes the mafia look like Boy Scouts.

Yes, it's time for an Amber Alert. Our country has been stolen. The only question is, will Amber Alert even work, or will Obama disable the system?

NSA collects millions of e-mail address books globally

By Barton Gellman and Ashkan Soltani, Washington Post

.The collection program, which has not been disclosed before, intercepts e-mail address books and "buddy lists" from instant messaging services as they move across global data links. Online services often transmit those contacts when a user logs on, composes a message, or synch The National Security Agency is harvesting hundreds of millions of contact lists from personal e-mail and instant messaging accounts around the world, many of them belonging to Americans, according to senior intelligence officials and top-secret documents provided by former NSA contractor Edward Snowdenronizes a computer or mobile device with information stored on remote servers.

Rather than targeting individual users, the NSA is gathering contact lists in large numbers that amount to a sizable fraction of the world's e-mail and instant messaging accounts. Analysis of that data enables the agency to search for hidden connections and to map relationships within a much smaller universe of foreign intelligence targets.

During a single day last year, the NSA's Special Source Operations branch collected 444,743 e-mail address books from Yahoo, 105,068 from Hotmail, 82,857 from Facebook, 33,697 from Gmail and 22,881 from unspecified other providers, according to an internal NSA PowerPoint presentation. Those figures, described as a typical daily intake in the document, correspond to a rate of more than 250 million a year.

Each day, the presentation said, the NSA collects contacts from an estimated 500,000 buddy lists on live-chat services as well as from the inbox displays of Web-based e-mail accounts.

The collection depends on secret arrangements with foreign telecommunications companies or allied intelligence services in control of facilities that direct traffic along the Internet's main data routes.

Although the collection takes place overseas, two senior U.S. intelligence officials acknowledged that it sweeps in the contacts of many Americans. They declined to offer an estimate but did not dispute that the number is likely to be in the millions or tens of millions.

A spokesman for the Office of the Director of National Intelligence, which oversees the NSA, said the agency "is focused on discovering and developing intelligence about valid foreign intelligence targets like terrorists, human traffickers and drug smugglers. We are not interested in personal information about ordinary Americans."

The spokesman, Shawn Turner, added that rules approved by the attorney general require the NSA to "minimize the acquisition, use and dissemination" of information that identifies a U.S. citizen or permanent resident.

The NSA's collection of nearly all U.S. call records, under a separate program, has generated significant controversy since it was revealed in June. The NSA's director, Gen. Keith B. Alexander, has defended "bulk" collection as an essential counterterrorism and foreign intelligence tool, saying, "You need the haystack to find the needle."

Contact lists stored online provide the NSA with far richer sources of data than call records alone. Address books commonly include not only names and e-mail addresses, but also telephone numbers, street addresses, and business and family information. Inbox listings of e-mail accounts stored in the "cloud" sometimes contain content, such as the first few lines of a message.

Taken together, the data would enable the NSA, if permitted, to draw detailed maps of a person's life, as told by personal, professional, political and religious connections. The picture can also be misleading, creating false "associations" with ex-spouses or people with whom an account holder has had no contact in many years.

The NSA has not been authorized by Congress or the special intelligence court that oversees foreign surveillance to collect contact lists in bulk, and senior intelligence officials said it would be illegal to do so from facilities in the United States. The agency avoids the restrictions in the Foreign Intelligence Surveillance Act by intercepting contact lists from access points "all over the world," one official said, speaking on the condition of anonymity to discuss the classified program. "None of those are on U.S. territory."

Because of the method employed, the agency is not legally required or technically able to restrict its intake to contact lists belonging to specified foreign intelligence targets, he said.

When information passes through "the overseas collection apparatus," the official added; "the assumption is you're not a U.S. person."

In practice, data from Americans is collected in large volumes — in part because they live and work overseas, but also because data crosses international boundaries even when its American owners stay at home. Large technology companies, including Google and Facebook, maintain data centers around the world to balance loads on their servers and work around outages.

A senior U.S. intelligence official said the privacy of Americans is protected, despite mass collection, because "we have checks and balances built into our tools."

NSA analysts, he said, may not search within the contacts database or distribute information from it unless they can "make the case that something in there is a valid foreign intelligence target in and of itself."

In this program, the NSA is obliged to make that case only to itself or others in the executive branch. With few exceptions, intelligence operations overseas fall solely within the president's legal purview. The Foreign Intelligence Surveillance Act, enacted in 1978, imposes restrictions only on electronic surveillance that targets Americans or takes place on U.S. territory.

By contrast, the NSA draws on authority in the Patriot Act for its bulk collection of domestic phone records, and it gathers online records from U.S. Internet companies, in a program known as PRISM, under powers granted by Congress in the FISA Amendments Act. Those operations are overseen by the Foreign Intelligence Surveillance Court.

Sen. Dianne Feinstein, the California Democrat who chairs the Senate Intelligence Committee, said in August that the committee has less information about, and conducts less oversight of, intelligence gathering that relies solely on presidential authority. She said she planned to ask for more briefings on those programs.

"In general, the committee is far less aware of operations conducted under 12333," said a senior committee staff member, referring to Executive Order 12333, which defines the basic powers and responsibilities of the intelligence agencies. "I believe the NSA would answer questions if we asked them, and if we knew to ask them, but it would not routinely report these things, and, in general, they would not fall within the focus of the committee."

Because the agency captures contact lists "on the fly" as they cross major Internet switches, rather than "at rest" on computer servers, the NSA has no need to notify the U.S. companies that host the information or to ask for help from them.

"We have neither knowledge of, nor participation. in this mass collection of web-mail addresses or chat lists by the government," said Google spokeswoman Niki Fenwick.

At Microsoft, spokeswoman Nicole Miller said the company "does not provide any government with direct or unfettered access to our customers' data," adding that "we would have significant concerns if these allegations about government actions are true."

Facebook spokeswoman Jodi Seth said that "we did not know and did not assist" in the NSA's interception of contact lists.

It is unclear why the NSA collects more than twice as many address books from Yahoo than the other big services combined. One possibility is that Yahoo, unlike other service providers, has left connections to its users unencrypted by default.

Suzanne Philion, a Yahoo spokeswoman, said Monday in response to an inquiry from The Washington Post that, beginning in January, Yahoo would begin encrypting all its e-mail connections.

Google was the first to secure all its e-mail connections, turning on "SSL encryption" globally in 2010. People with inside knowledge said the move was intended in part to thwart large-scale collection of its users' information by the NSA and other intelligence agencies.

The volume of NSA contacts collection is so high that it has occasionally threatened to overwhelm storage repositories, forcing the agency to halt its intake with "emergency detasking" orders. Three NSA documents describe short-term efforts to build an "across-the-board technology throttle for truly heinous data" and longer-term efforts to filter out information that the NSA does not need.

Spam has proven to be a significant problem for the NSA — clogging databases with information that holds no foreign intelligence value. The majority of all e-mails, one NSA document says, "are SPAM from 'fake' addresses and never 'delivered' to targets."

In fall 2011, according to an NSA presentation, the Yahoo account of an Iranian target was "hacked by an unknown actor," who used it to send spam. The Iranian had "a number of Yahoo groups in his/her contact list, some with many hundreds or thousands of members."

The cascading effects of repeated spam messages, compounded by the automatic addition of the Iranian's contacts to other people's address books, led to a massive spike in the volume of traffic collected by the Australian intelligence service on the NSA's behalf.

After nine days of data-bombing, the Iranian's contact book and contact books for several people within it were "emergency de-tasked."

In a briefing from the NSA's Large Access Exploitation working group, that example was used to illustrate the need to narrow the criteria for data interception. It called for a "shifting collection philosophy": "Memorialize what you need" vs. "Order one of everything off the menu and eat what you want."

Congress and this administration are out of control, and have been for years. There are children hungry in the U.S., yet those in Congress get free haircuts. Next time you talk to your Congressman, ask why we go from war-to-war, and why the people in Congress are out of touch with the American people? As long as they get their pay and perks – they don't care!

America's Fundamental Transformation Under Obama

Monica Crowley

Monica Crowley, Ph.D., is a Fox News Contributor, host of the nationally syndicated "Monica Crowley Show," and the author of What the (Bleep) Just Happened? The Happy Warrior's Guide to the Great American Comeback.

Last week on "The O'Reilly Factor," I recalled how Barack Obama spoke in 2008 about the "fundamental transformation of the nation." After five years of his presidency, we see the enormous success he's had in achieving it.

The objective was always to move America away from a nation built on individual liberty and economic freedom and toward a government welfare and dependency state. Socialism, communism, statism, leftism — in the end it doesn't matter what you call it, because what matters is what's being carried out…and its consequences.

U.S. President Barack Obama speaks about Affordable Care Act at The Fairmont Hotel on June 6, 2013 in San Jose, California (Photo Credit: Getty Images)

Radical wealth redistribution, class warfare, socialized medicine, the atomization of American society, divisive identity politics, the war on success, the loss of our Triple A credit rating, the retrenchment of U.S. power abroad, the gutting of our military, the erosion of our international credibility.

It's all being done deliberately by Obama and the left in order to "fundamentally transform" this country into just another crippled dependency state.

After five years of evidence, people are still wondering aloud why Obama doesn't negotiate, why he doesn't compromise, why he doesn't handle things the way, say, Bill Clinton did.

Wake the BLEEP up! (and by the way, my book laid all of this out and more. Please see the top of this website for how to order the paperback edition of "What The (Bleep) Just Happened?" It's all there…and way ahead of its time.)

Unlike Clinton, who was a pragmatist, Obama is a pure ideologue. Why do you think he hasn't negotiated with Republicans? First, it's because he doesn't really have to, given that the liberals in Congress and the media protect and advance his interests at every turn and because the GOP is so spineless. Second, it's because he's a total ideologue who will never give anything on his way to "fundamentally transforming the nation."

Guess what Obama's next move is? Pushing for immigration "reform" (see the story here). Why? Because granting amnesty to tens of millions of illegals, locking them into government dependency, and creating a permanent Democrat voting majority is the final, missing piece of the "fundamental transformation of the nation."

After that, America is over.

Stop waiting for Obama to change. It's never going to happen. And while we're over here, contemplating our navels and whining about his unwillingness to compromise, he and the left are busily remaking America — right from under us.

Is it too late? I don't know. Maybe. I wish I could be more optimistic. But the "leadership" on our side is completely unready and unwilling to wage this fight. They simply aren't up to it.

President Barack Obama meets with small business owners about the government shutdown and debt ceiling, Friday, Oct. 11, 2013, in the Roosevelt Room of the White House in Washington. (Photo Credit: AP)

And while we've got a few brave souls on the Hill who get it and are fearlessly fighting back — guys like Senators Ted Cruz and Mike Lee — the Left has been working tirelessly (along with disgraceful members of the GOP as well) to marginalize and discredit them.

Meanwhile, the left — flanked by its troops in the media — keeps pressing and pressing, exhausting us until we give up, while they never rest, never falter, never compromise, and never fail.

And, well, we're losing. Not just the fights over the CR and the debt ceiling and Obamacare, but the future of the country. That doesn't mean that we should stop fighting. We must fight with every breath and ounce of energy we've got. But we need to understand what we're up against, how far down the road of "transformation" we already are, and how our own leadership is failing us.

It's time to regroup and re-energize and maybe even re-brand the Tea Party. It's time to find and recruit real conservatives to run for office, from the bottom up. It's time to support folks who are doing that, from Heritage to FreedomWorks.

It's time for our own "fundamental transformation." Let's go.

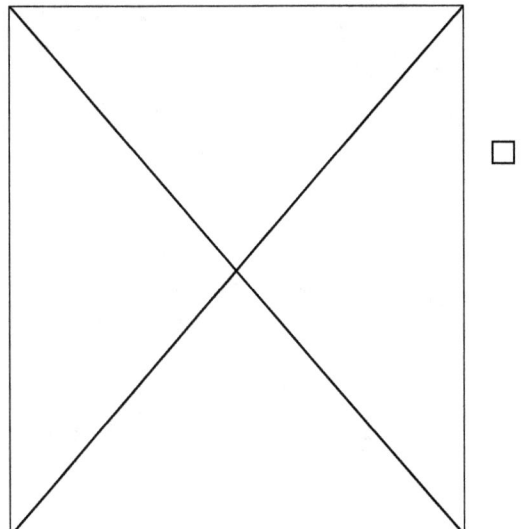

www.ingramcontent.com/pod-product-compliance
Lightning Source LLC
Chambersburg PA
CBHW070805290526
45795CB00002B/638